Xmas   2014

The Beauty of Everyday Life

Happy CHRISTMAS
Dad
HopE You ENJOY

The Beauty
of Everyday Life

Stories in Honour of Teen-Line Ireland

Compiled and edited
by
Adrian Millar

The Beauty of Everyday Life
Stories in Honour of Teen-Line Ireland
Compiled and edited by Adrian Millar

Cover photo courtesy of Mike O'Toole **www.mikeotoole.com**

Cover design, page layout, and typesetting courtesy of
Martine Maguire-Weltecke **www.mmw-design.com**

ISBN 978-1-326-03731-4

In memory of a beautiful teenager

Frédérique Albizzati

CONTENTS

Contents

ACKNOWLEDGEMENTS

For anything to get done in life, you need good friends. I would like to thank my good friend James Froggatt for his constant encouragement over the years with my writing "jigsaw". I would also like to thank my friends Micky and Lorna Timmons for being behind me all the way. Brendan Moran, Andy Kilty and Mike O'Toole are my day-to-day friends who have encouraged me on a daily basis with this book – my thanks to them. Peter Hannan has helped me see the beauty in my life and the bigger Christian vision within which it unfolds, and I am grateful for that. Mary Jenkinson O'Connor has been there all the way for me along with my friend Pauline O'Connor, both of them constantly listening and encouraging me in life. Many friends have lent me an ear to prod me onwards with this book: thanks to Fiona Gallagher, Iain Atack, Angela Tunney, Alice and Brendan Gorman, Luise Wirthe, Eric and Sinead Reid, Cathy Judge, Katrin and Sean Millar, Jackie and Brendan Curtis, Barbara McAllister, Conor McHugh, Noel Daly, Tony Doorey, Pádraicín Ní Mhurchú, Deirdre Molloy, Mary Thornton, Katia Bulat, Jacques Albizzati, Aidan O'Callaghan and Deirdre Curtis. This book would never have happened without my friend Tony O'Riordan who helped me identify the beauty of everyday life as my central passion in life and got me working on this.

My thanks also to Jackie Gallagher of Q4PR who has been there countless times for me on my writing journey and whose idea this book was, to Angie Kinane of Q4PR who sent me in the right direction, to Nora Lawton of Weber Shandwick, to Vinney Murphy, to Sean Closkey, to Gerry O' Beirne, to Declan Brennan, to Niall Cronin, and to Patricia Whelton who put me in touch with several

Acknowledgements

contributors to this book. A very special word of thanks goes to to Martine Maguire-Weltecke of mmw-design.com for putting her excellent design and typesetting skills to work in the creation of this book, free of charge. As you can see, it's a beautiful copy. Brian Langan of Transworld has always been there for me, helping me crystallise my writing vision, for which I am most grateful. I also extend my thanks to all the fine contributors to this book for giving so generously of their time and energies. It has been a pleasure working with you. I am delighted that this book is going out on behalf of Teen-Line Ireland which does such extraordinary work with young, vulnerable people.

Finally, I would like to thank my three daughters Aisling, Rebecca and Ciara, for their support in daily life. I am always grateful for them, whether I am writing or not.

My wife, Mary Deasy, is the love of my life. Who could ask for more? I'm a lucky man.

Adrian Millar

FOREWORD

Maureen Bolger

Founder and Director, Teen-Line Ireland

My 16-year-old son Darren brought love and laughter into my life from the moment I held him on February 19th, 1987. He came into this world crying like a little kitten and so I gave him the pet name "my kitty cat". He made me smile every day. Not just one day, but for the little time he had on this planet – 16 years – he would hold me and say 'I love you, Mam. You are the best Mam in the whole world' and I would reply 'I love you up the sky' and he would say back 'And around the corner' and we would both laugh. He loved to play the fool and make everyone laugh – my little joker, my little pal. We would watch TV on my bed most nights, our arms wrapped around each other watching Father Ted and Only Fools and Horses. I loved his laugh and the way he would mimic Father Ted, Father Jack, Mrs. Doyle and, of course, Father Dougal.

I do not know why my beautiful child took his own life on April 6th, 2003, but I will always remember his love for me and sometimes I smile at all the wonderful memories I have today of him and I am very proud of his legacy in the form of Teen-Line Ireland – a safe place for teenagers to talk and be listened to.

Teen-Line Ireland is a registered charity which provides a national, freephone, non-directive helpline service for teenagers who may be feeling alone, worried or distressed. The helpline is open seven days a week from 8pm to 11pm, with an extended service on Wednesdays from 4pm to 11pm.

Teenagers can ring and speak to a trained volunteer who will listen to them with empathy, respect and compassion. We also run a Teen-Line Schools Programme to build awareness of our helpline service. All funding for our services comes solely from donations and fundraising activities. If you wish to donate to Teen-Line Ireland, you can do so by donating directly through our AIB account:

Allied Irish Bank
Main Street, Tallaght, Dublin 24, Ireland.
Account no.: 12675468
Sort code: 93-33-17
BIC: AIBKIE2D
IBAN: IE14AIBK93331712675468

I will never forget my special Angel.

I love you, Darren, up the sky … and around the corner.

xxxxx

INTRODUCTION

Adrian Millar

My teenage daughter and I go for a walk by the Grand Canal.

'Daddy, what's The Beauty Of Everyday Life book all about?' she asks.

'It's about the stuff that we normally take for granted – the little things,' I say. 'A moment with our children, an encounter with a friend, a hand we held, a hug we exchanged, little incidents, love, relationships, friendship. That sort of thing.'

'I know what you mean, Daddy,' she says.

Does she, I'm thinking. How can a teenager really grasp the everyday stuff when their lives are so fast and furious?

'It's like the five euro note you find in your pocket that you never knew you had,' she says, 'like happened to me the other day. When you find it, you feel completely differently about your whole day. It's like 'Oh, wow, this is great!' even though it's the tiniest little thing.'

She could knock me over with a feather – or even with a picture of Josh Hutcherson, her latest Hollywood heart-throb, if she were crazy enough to waste one of those on me, which I doubt.

'That's exactly what the beauty of everyday life is!' I say. 'I would never have thought of that. Maybe you should be writing this book, instead of me, seeing as you are the one with all the wisdom.'

'Maybe, but it'll cost you, Daddy.'

'I'll have to think about that,' I say, laughing. 'You're amazing!'

"I know. Talent, daddy. Talent."

"But, of course, you get that from me."

She laughs, at my expense.

But she is right, I realise: the beauty of everyday life is about seeing the everyday things afresh.

'Daddy, so, how do you do keep in touch with the beauty of everyday life?' she asks, confidently flicking her long red hair back behind her shoulders now.

'By tapping into the 90% that is beautiful.'

'And how do you do that?'

'By noticing the richness of your everyday experience and putting words on it, then savouring it and sharing it – on Facebook; or wherever. Even just simply with your friends.'

'But what about the 10%, Daddy?'

Leave it to a teenager to go straight to the point, I'm thinking.

'Well, when you listen to the 10% that is difficult or painful, you are actually on the path to joy.'

'Oh, right, so, you recommend pain, do you, Daddy?'

I take a deep breath. I am dealing with a 14-year-old here, I remind myself. I was the same once myself. Blunt.

'No. I'm not recommending pain. What I'm saying is that when you face whatever's bothering you or troubling you, when you bring it in from the cold, it brings you to another level. It allows you to engage more fully with people and with life.'

'Mmmh ...' she says, unconvinced.

The jury is out on my philosophy of life.

I have to work harder, I realise. Besides, I think, she is right to put pressure on me to put my philosophy into my own words. One's convictions about the beauty of life are embedded deep beneath the surface of our everyday; you have to dig deep to bring them to the surface, and when you do, you never regret it for they remain your friend and guide for life

'What I mean is, it's the struggles in life that make us heroes ...'

'Heroines, Daddy. Just saying.'

'Heroines. And storytellers and lovers, and mystics and poets ...'

'Poetesses, Daddy.'

'And poetesses, and prophets ...'

'Prophetesses ...'

'OK, OK, you get my drift. It's the struggles that makes us human. But we don't like to show the vulnerable side of ourselves to people.'

'YOU KNOW WHAT, DADDY, YOU'RE A GENIUS,' she says.

I still haven't decided if my daughter was being sarcastic that day. What I do know is that the stories in this book capture the beauty of everyday life wonderfully. They were written by people who over the years have shone a light in our lives through their words and deeds and who have inspired us or entertained us. They will make you laugh, cry and reflect, but above all else they will remind you of the beauty of your own everyday life and inspire you to live it ever more fully.

I hope you enjoy them. They were written for you.

JOE DUFFY

Joe Duffy is the presenter of Liveline on RTÉ Radio 1.
He lives in Dublin.

My "Summer County" Complex

Mother would never let "Summer County" cross the door, let alone grace our kitchen table.

After all it was "margarine".

So, of a Thursday, when money was running low, very low, and it still being a day and a night away from my father's weekly wage packet, we would be despatched to Ruane's Shop for a quarter-pound of butter – not the much cheaper, half-pound of "Summer County". Never Ever. To be seen with margarine would be mortification – an indication of inability to cope, like waving a white flag to the poverty that was constantly knocking at the hall door. As if I would draw attention to myself running the short distance from our house on one side of Claddagh Green to the shop on the other, doing a three-hand reel with the dreaded gold foil-wrapped, exotically titled margarine – at least the quarter of butter was wrapped discreetly in greaseproof paper, and hidden.

Bizarrely, Mother seemed to lose her fear of social embarrassment when it came to the dreaded trips to the turf depot – a trip that involved a three-mile trek through the centre of Ballyfermot with my little brother Aidan's pram laden with teetering sacks of wet turf. A marching band in full flight would attract less attention than me and my younger brother Peter trying to manhandle Aidan's pram up Ballyfermot Road, which in truth is a long, punishing steep hill rather than an innocuous road. Not only did she drop all social pretence when it came to the quest for turf, she seemed to forget other basic principles of family life which I firmly held to – such as the eldest should be called on first for the heavy jobs. This was probably because James, our eldest, was already working with my father in Glen Abbey Hosiery and handing up his unopened brown wage packet every Friday – and so was granted an amnesty from this back-breaking, public toil. And of course everyone knew that to go to the turf depot was a sign that times were tough in your house: after all, only poor old-age pensioners were given "turf dockets", which is where we got ours – our Nana Murphy being the entitled bearer of the handwritten yellow bits of paper grandly titled "Fuel Vouchers" entitling the bearer to one hundredweight of turf. This docket gave our family heat and life, but instilled nothing but dread into my heart because I knew that once the docket was safely placed in Mother's purse it would not be long before she would noisily drag Aidan's pram from its parking spot under the stairs, throw the two empty coal-sacks in and call myself and Peter to order, before nonchalantly ordering us to the turf depot with a rider that not a single sod was to be lost by theft or negligence on the way back.

I refuse to believe that the same woman who saw nothing but embarrassment in being seen with a half pound of foil-wrapped margarine was immune to the stigma of her two young sons wrestling with two four-stone, carbuncled, dirty sacks of turf stacked high on their baby brother's pram, pushing and willing it three miles up Ballyfermot's main road. The Saint Patrick's Day parade going up O'Connell Street would crane fewer necks and turn fewer heads.

While the run to the turf depot on Lally Road was long, it was downhill, after all, and the pram was empty, but still our hearts filled with fear once we turned right on to O'Hogan Road because it was then that you would see the length of the queue. Hundreds of other – and bigger – kids standing there with every class of vehicle from boxcar to bicycle, all queuing for the turf. Not only was it the fear of being beaten up by these kids who might discover that we were from the 'top end' of the scheme that sent our hearts racing –

it was the prospect of a wasted journey if the turf ran out before we got to the top of the queue.

And so we stood, silently, fuming, fearful, as the queue of wheeled contraptions snaked its way up Lally Road to the turf depot. The depot, by the way, was no more than a yard with an antiquated weighing scales on a wooden frame at its centre. When we got to the top of the queue we would hand over our golden docket to the shovel-man who would heave the appropriate cast iron metal weight onto the scales. Shovelling turf in the open-mouthed metal scoop, you were instructed to hold your coal-sack as the gangly unruly sods flew in every direction – except into your sack. It was like trying to wrestle an octopus into a net bag. You would be laughed at, sneered and jeered as myself and Peter – amateurs – scrambled to fill the sacks and manhandle them onto the pram. We scurried off as quickly as possible, shaking off any potential cowboys from the lower end of the scheme who might attempt to rustle our precious pile.

The most difficult part of the climb was the beginning. It was not just the steep hill that challenged us; we would be humiliated if by chance any of our teachers were leaving our school as we skulked past, for surely they would spot us trying to roll our boulder, like Sisyphus, up the unending Ballyfermot hill.

Peter and I would take turns gripping and pushing the white rubber-clad handle of the pram – the effort rendered us almost horizontal – while the other would push from the side and stop it from rolling back down the hill, but neither of us could let up or let go.

We beat a steady path, shifting from the shadows only once when "go-be-the-wall", the local walking book-reader, headed straight, and refused to deviate as always, in our direction.

And we dared not give up. We always did what Mother told us since the time she caught myself and Peter mitching from school – well, actually, we gave ourselves up after two hours of boredom – our stuttering excuse that the school was closed expiring within seconds as Mother's instinct reduced us to a pair of blubbering truth-tellers. Propelling us up the stairs to our bedrooms by the robust application of a wooden spoon to the back of our legs was an effective – and memorable – sanction. And so we could not even contemplate surrender. We did our best. Gathering extra wind as we got to the main row of shops, not because of a nasty incline but because it was where the Duffy brothers were most likely to be spotted by passing neighbours on the top deck of the 78 bus home.

Neither was our arrival home worthy of remark by either our mother or siblings. For myself and Peter, we had just completed a feat comparable only to Edmund Hillery and Tenzing Norgay ascending Mount Everest thirteen years previously – except they had more oxygen.

After emptying the sacks of turf into the coal-shed, Peter and I would clean out Aidan's pram, and as sure as anything, Mother would remind us that we were not to go out to play without the pram and its rightful occupant in tow.

This lack of gratitude baffled us no end.

Mother, now in her 85th year, still remembers and abides by the "Summer County" fatwa but has no recollection of our epic turf expeditions. Unremarked upon then – and now. A life lesson.

You see, Mother believes the greater gift of humility and the lesson that life can be hard, but bearable, comes from overcoming the bigger challenge.

Sure who would notice a young fella carrying a half-pound of Summer County margarine anyway?

ANGIE BENHAFFAF

Angie Benhaffaf is mother to Ireland's beloved conjoined twins Hassan and Hussein Benhaffaf – also affectionately known as "Ireland's Little Fighters". The twins were born on 2nd December 2009 and later separated at Great Ormond Street Hospital in London April 2010. The twins shared everything except the heart and miraculously survived a 14-hour surgery to separate them. They were sadly left with one leg each and are now learning to walk with prosthetic legs or 'superman legs' as the twins call them. Hassan and Hussein continue to have ongoing surgeries and constant physio/hospital appoint-ments but they always remind us that courage, hope and un-conditional love is the true meaning of family.

Ireland's Little Fighters
(Miracles still happen and dreams do come true)

My precious children Hassan and Hussein opened my eyes to the wonderful world we live in. Over the past four years I have cried till I can cry no more as the pain of watching my twin boys struggle through everyday life. They don't cry, they laugh, they smile and they love life. And, boy, does life love them back! They've survived the impossible so many times and from the time I saw them clasping hands in my 3D scan at 24 weeks gestation, I knew these were my "little fighters".

During the toughest times of our lives my husband Azzedine and I found humour, and that's what helped get us through the emotional roller coaster. The funniest thing was when the boys were about 8 weeks old and still conjoined and we received two hospital appointments by post. Hassan's appointment was at 2:30pm and Hussein's appointment was at 3pm. I remember reading it twice and cheekily telling Azzedine that I might ring up the hospital and tell them Hussein can't make it that day.

At another hospital appointment, still prior to the boys' separation, the receptionist asked us "Are they both going in?" You tell me, I felt like saying. Yes, if we didn't laugh we would cry.

My precious little two older girls have had an extremely tough few years with the trauma and upset of what their little brothers have gone through and are still going through. But all in all I have never seen a love as strong and when they ask me to teach them how to put on their brothers' 'superman legs' so that they can help them and help me, I know I've done something right.

What fills my heart with strength is that we started out this journey as a family of six and thankfully we continue it as a family of six. Malika, my eldest child, looks after me and loves me so much. She gives me a hug when I need it most. Iman, my other little girl, makes us laugh at times we never thought we could laugh. And my boys, my precious boys, have given us and so many others HOPE. Even in our darkest hour it is so important to cling on to some hope. Hassan and Hussein have reminded us all of the important things in life, and I see the world so differently since they were born. They were a 'gift' sent from above and as tough as life is they are the happiest little duo you will ever meet. They would be entitled to be agitated or short tempered after all they've gone through and will continue to go through, but they're not! They are full of fun, full of mischief and full of life. They know how precious life is and that's why they live each day to the fullest.

I feel that at the start of our journey, at our first scan, after we found out that they were conjoined and that they had no chance of survival, my heart actually broke, but somehow I had to put it back together again.

Then, to love them and get to know them for four months and hand them over for separation was impossible, knowing that one or both could die. Every part of me told me to pick them up and run and not to hand them over. They were a perfect heart shape and I felt I was allowing them to be torn apart. No parent should have to go through something like this. Life is so precious!

These boys fought to live and, thank God, survived a 14-hour surgery to separate them. They had shared everything except the heart, even the pericardium sac around the heart, but still they survived. We feel blessed with them and they bring happiness wherever they go. I think that even when they're older they will still be called 'Ireland's Little Fighters' and I know they are here for a reason.

We will be forever grateful to all the people who prayed for our boys and supported us through the toughest times of our lives. The boys just bring out the best in everyone and remind us all of the important things in life: love, happiness and above all HOPE.

I have made life-long friends through this whole experience and these friends are precious to me. Hassan and Hussein are living proof that miracles still happen and dreams do come true.

Finally, I'd like to share with you a poem that I wrote in my months of heartache leading up to my precious boys' separation through surgery.

I loved you both from the very start,
When doctors thought you shared one heart.
I cried so much during that time;
we did not think that all would be fine.
Your two big sisters got me through the worst.
I really felt that I had been cursed.
For eight months I was in such a lonely place
as the birth was something I thought I couldn't face.
But then came that beautiful winter's morn,
on the 2nd December my 'little fighters' were born.
To hear you both cry was music to our ears,
Your dad and I cried so many tears.
You both have given me courage and strength,
what a wonderful 'gift' we have been sent!
'Hassan' is the quiet one and a minute older,
'Hussein' is the naughty one – he's a little bit bolder!
Two wonderful boys joined together in love,

You truly are a gift sent from above.
I feel so honoured to be your mum,
I need just one more miracle to come.
'The Little Fighters' is the name ye share,
You have earned it well, as you fought to be here.
Your final battle is getting near,
We are all behind you so have no fear.
Boys, you have filled us all with love and hope,
without you both we would never cope.
Keep on fighting to stay strong
and always remember your big sisters' song.
'You are not alone' is the song they sing for you,
and those words could not be more true!
So as we prepare for the surgery ahead,
many a tear will be shed.
All I can ask of God now is that you feel no pain,
I'm so proud of my boys, Hassan and Hussein.
No matter how this will all end,
I am forever grateful for the time we did spend.
You have brought the country together, in love and prayer,
You have made 2010 a special year!
Always remember 'You are not alone'
Please God someday, we'll all return home.
I feel I must be one of the luckiest mums,
To have not one, but two precious sons.

Love you both with all my heart & soul,
Mummy xx

NIALL BRESLIN ('BRESSIE')

Singer, songwriter, producer and performer, Niall Breslin was a member of one of Ireland's biggest rock 'n' roll bands, The Blizzards, before turning solo in 2010. He is a judge on RTÉ's The Voice.

The Swim

One trait I feel every human being on the planet has in common is that we all either rationally or irrationally have a phobia. Whether we like to admit it or not, there is always something in-built in everyone's subconscious that generates fear. Many of my mates swear they have no fears, for as a society we all view vulnerability as a weakness, but if I peg a black widow spider in their face I am sure their macho persona would momentarily evade them.

The reason I speak of phobias is that I myself have suffered for years with a crippling phobia of the one most important and abundant resource in the world, "WATER". Not drinking it of course but swimming in it. I hated everything about water. It's cold; there are fish in there (which is another less crippling phobia of mine, but having swum in the Irish sea, that is changing. Very, very ugly fish in there!), I have a big arse that's like the titanic and constantly wants to sink, making swimming much more difficult, and finally, of course, you can drown in it.

I do not know where this fear came from but even when my mother tried to bath me as a baby on a Saturday night I would shatter glass with the screams out of me. This phobia has stopped me for many years from doing things I really wish I could do.

Having suffered with mental health issues, I know that the one common denominator surrounding those affected by such issues is the complete frustration of not being able to control and manage your own mind and head. My phobia of water and my ability to overcome this fear ironically has had a massive impact on my ability to control my mental health issues. Let me explain.

At Xmas 2012 I spent five days in bed unable to converge or communicate with anyone due to my mental state of mind. While lying in bed I made a promise to myself that in 2013 I was going to take on and fight back against my anxiety.

I decided to sign up for my first triathlon which of course includes an open water swim.

Now, up to this point in my life, due to my phobia, I was unable to swim. So, I had to undertake months of training in a pool to learn how to swim and more importantly learn how to stay calm in the water. My swim coach Carole was amazing and understood and was very sensitive to my irrational phobia. I can easily say I dreaded the thought of getting into the pool each day. What I dreaded even more, however, was the thought of an open water swim in a deep lake surrounded by 300-400 other swimmers.

Fast forward a few months to my first triathlon which took place in Lanesboro in Co. Longford. Putting on my wetsuit and looking out into the open water in which I would be racing I felt my body come close to one of my well oiled and frequent panic attacks, but something in my head stopped it. My good friend Derry said he would swim beside me all the way, which helped. As I stepped into the water I remember it was almost a relief as the air temperature was 28 degrees and I was melting, so the cold water cooled me down as I awaited the starting gun. When the gun went off, the water exploded as if from a mackerel dash as the 300 swimmers fought for space up the front. I just positioned myself at the back where I thought I would get in no one's way. Approximately three minutes into the swim Derry looked up to see myself and another swimmer boxing the head of each other in the water as the 'prick' kept grabbing my foot to pull me under the water. As our little tiff settled down I started concentrating on my stroke even though all that was going through my head was the thought of the deep lake that I was swimming in out in open water. Again the panic tried to creep back but something stopped it and I kept concentrating on my stroke. Then about half way through the swim something truly remarkable happened. As my fellow swimmers huffed and puffed through their long swim I started smiling. A sense of complete triumph came over me. Not because I was doing well in the race but because this crippling phobia suddenly was removed from my life and at that point for the first time I can remember I realised one thing: I HAVE CONTROL OF MY MIND, IT DOES NOT CONTROL ME.

Getting out of the water to take on the bike leg of the race, my mates said I was the only person smiling, laughing even. To them, they just saw the surface: a guy enjoying the race and having fun, but underneath all that, I knew it was something much more profound. A guy that after years of struggling with mental health issues, phobias and panic attacks, a guy who never ever felt in control of his own mind, literally regaining his head and successfully going some way in taking on and beating the painful and difficult issues he has lived with all his life, and essentially letting his mind know who is the boss.

That night I went home a new man and committed and signed up to doing my first IRONMAN triathlon which I completed in May 2014 in Austria.

The beauty of everyday life is embracing chaos when it comes and accepting love when it's offered.

Don't be afraid to be vulnerable as without flaws we have no virtues.

GERRY ADAMS

Gerry Adams grew up in the Ballymurphy district of West Belfast. In 1983 he was elected President of Sinn Féin. He was also elected MP for West Belfast in the same year. He resigned from Westminster in 2011 and stood in the Louth constituency in the general election for the Irish Parliament. He topped the poll. Gerry is the author of 14 books, including: Falls Memories; A Pathway to Peace; The Politics of Irish Freedom *and* Selected Writings; A New Ireland – A Vision for the Future; *his autobiographies* Before the Dawn *and* Hope and History – Making Peace in Ireland; An Irish Voice *and* An Irish Journal.

The Beauty of Small Things

When I've been in hard places, I've always found it important not to get totally overwhelmed by events that life challenges you with. It's necessary to step outside of the particular issue, to feel the wind in your face, or watch the light as it changes in the sky. If you do this with nature, you will see the beauty in human beings too. I met a woman the other day who had lost a child in the Stardust fire disaster and had just buried another of her adult children. She was articulate and passionate and had learned a lot on her quest for justice. I couldn't but marvel at the beauty of her spirit. I also found this spirit in Fr. Alec Reid. Without him there would not have been an Irish Peace Process at the time it was created. I will always remember visiting him in the nursing home towards the end of his life, with a mutual friend, Lucilita Bhreathnach. The three of us walked through the streets of Dublin for an hour singing 'come-all-youse' – 'I'll Take You Home Again Kathleen', 'Biddy Mulligan The

Pride Of The Coombe', whatever tunes came into our heads. We were on a bit of a high, singing where we weren't supposed to, in the streets after dark. We were like school children. Not a drink taken. We didn't break breath when we passed strangers. It was hugely entertaining and uplifting. A beautiful bit of innocent fun between friends. Friendship is central to living a full life. Friends and friendship are beautiful.

Of course, other people in my life are beautiful too – my wife, our son, his wife, and our grandchildren – but beauty also comes to you through incidental encounters – a simple sentence from a stranger who has accumulated a lifetime's wisdom from their ancestors. You discover then that there are small things in life that are hugely important. And beautiful. More important than wealth or material possessions.

I have also found beauty at the saddest of times. At the funeral of Nelson Mandela, amidst the sense of deep loss, I found it particularly poignant that two hundred or so women sang spontaneously and danced the toi-toi in synchronisation, ignoring the appeals of the speakers on the podium. You have to laugh and celebrate – not in a false way – especially when things are tough. I learned the importance of this during the hard times in Belfast. I formed the opinion at funerals that my friend Fr. Des Wilson spoke at, that he was there to cheer us up, to give us hope. You can actually make hope. First you have to realise that you can bring about change. Out of that comes hope. I knew that the war in Ireland could be changed. There was a way out of it. Negotiations were needed. The problem was political. It needed political negotiation. We needed to change the conditions for others to move. Until that dawned on me my mantra was that the responsibility was on our critics to find an alternative way, but when you think of it, why should they? We had to find the alternative way ourselves. That's where Fr. Alec Reid came in: he never lost his great belief in humanity and in the Holy Spirit and in the way human beings have the ability to sort things out.

But let's not get too carried away. I live in the real world. In the real world, people get cranky and grumpy. But grumpiness has its good side also. I think Patrick Kavanagh encapsulated this beautifully.

He was by all accounts cantankerous but he wrote of blue-bells and love. Women are great, especially older working class women.
I have lots of women in my life. Maggie McArdle, my wife Colette's mother, like many of her generation reared ten children in hard times. She was wise and earthy and full of songs. My Granny Adams, who was very influential in my life had a wisdom, which she shared with the other women of her time who had large families and lived in a general atmosphere of poverty. It was a spirituality that was bigger than any institution. I think she passed something of this on to me. She also passed her love of flowers on to me. Thanks to her, I have a great affection for geraniums, montbretia, primroses and roses. And nature. Sometimes all it takes is for me to walk the dog out in the fields and I'm on a high, exhilarated.

In prison, you get a value of freedom. As a result, you come to see how lucky you are and how every day is blessed. Besides, if you are lucky enough to survive a conflict in which so many close friends were killed, you understand these blessings in an even more profound way. You understand the value of fun and humour too. You have got to absorb it. There is a great wisdom in acting the eejit. Never take yourself entirely too seriously, I think. Take your work seriously. Never lose your sense of outrage but stay grounded. If you are having fun, I always find that the adventure is greater with kids, given their love, imagination and innocence. The joys of strategic farting is an art, with young people.

In the wake of a conflict, I have also come to realise the critical importance of eschewing hatred. Hatred is corrosive. Why hate those who shot me, or those who slammed armoured personnel carriers into my mother's home? You have to snap out of negativity by looking for a solution, like Nelson Mandela did. This does not mean that you ignore the oppressor's injustice. I valued Mandela's hard-headedness in the face of his oppressor just as much as his ability to give. There is a beautiful strength in the human spirit that builds equality or a negotiated settlement with the oppressor. Hatred only gets in the way. The prize is great. I was at a function once in Hillsborough for Ian Paisley Snr. I remember coming across his wife Eileen sitting on her own. 'Can I join you?'

I said. 'Yes,' she said. There then followed an hour-long conversation about porridge, vegetables, dogs and children. Grace was coming out of it in abundance. It was a hugely important conversation – two human beings who had never talked before because of the war found out that they had so much in common.

I have a brilliant and inspirational friend who lives in the 'nowness' of the everyday. His name is Donnacha Rynne. He is a young man with profound disabilities. Donnacha is loveable and compassionate, but tough so that he can get through every day. He has strength of spirit.

I think that there is a lesson in that for all of us. To live life well, you have to have strength. I hope you find it.

Beir Bua! Live life!

FRANCES BLACK

Frances Black was born in Dublin. She began singing with her older siblings, Shay, Michael, Mary, and Martin, known as The Black Family, *when she was 17. She has twice been the recipient of one of the highest honours in Irish music, the prestigious Irish Recorded Music Association's Best Irish Female Award. Alongside the music, Frances's other main passion in life is The Rise Foundation, a charitable organisation that she founded herself, which is dedicated to assisting families in understanding the nature of the disease of addiction, and the profound effects it has on relationships.*

Letter to My Dad

Hi Dad, it's been a long time since we talked. Sometimes it feels like only yesterday, and yet it's been 23 years since you passed. I want to say thank you for the beautiful memories that you gave me as a child. The wonderful holidays that we had when we went to the stunning island that you were born and reared on, Rathlin Island.

I am not saying that life was perfect for us by any means – I know times were hard for both you and Mam rearing five kids in the inner city of Dublin, but somehow we got by, didn't we?

My favourite memory is when I was 16. You had retired from your work as a plasterer a few years earlier, and you and Mam decided to open up a small grocer's shop on Charlemont Street. At that time, you also had very bad arthritis and needed someone to travel with you on a trip back to your homestead on Rathlin.

It was the end of July and I was so thrilled that you asked me to go with you. Mam couldn't go due to work commitments with the shop. I was the youngest of the family and the others were either working or away.

Do you remember, Dad, that you wanted to stop off at Auntie Maggie's house in Loughinisland, Co Down, on the way to Rathlin? We had no car, so we got the bus to Newry, and then another one to Newcastle, Co Down.

We missed the bus to Downpatrick, so you found a lovely B&B on the seafront where the landlady cooked us a meal of steak and mushroom pie. I had never tasted anything like it before.

Afterwards, we took a short walk on the seafront, and I asked you questions about the British Army trucks going up and down the street.

I couldn't understand what they were doing in this beautiful seaside town, and I had never seen soldiers with guns pointed before. When you started to explain it to me, I knew by the way you spoke about the conflict that it brought you huge sadness. I could see the sorrow in your eyes.

The funny thing was, even though it was at the height of the conflict, not once did I feel in any way scared because I was with you.

We watched the news that night and saw that three Catholic civilians were killed as a result of a bomb attack on Andersonstown Road, and an off-duty RUC officer was killed by a British soldier following an argument at a checkpoint in Bessbrook, Co Armagh. I watched you walk up to your room that night with a heavy heart.

The next day, we headed up to see Auntie Maggie in Loughinisland, where you spent three days talking with her and having cups of tea, and I helped Charlie (who worked for Auntie Maggie) and Charlie's daughter to work on the farm.

I will never forget the dinners that Auntie Maggie cooked. Everything that was on the dinner plate was straight from the farm. The potatoes were balls of white fluff and, with the homemade butter, they melted in your mouth. There was a lot of laughter when she was around. I could see that you really admired her and looked up to her. She was so wise and gentle.

By the time we got to Rathlin Island, the weather was beautiful. The journey on the boat over was rough. There was a huge swell on the sea as we travelled with your very dear friend Danny Hannaway.

Danny had a boat; he was another islander who had married a Dublin woman. Her name was Carmel. They were such a lovely couple with a lovely family.

When we arrived on Rathlin, there was a car waiting to bring us up to the family farm, 'Glacklugh'. Your eldest brother Michael and your sister Mary were waiting and had the warmest greeting that you could have imagined – lots of shaking hands and smiling with warm words of welcome. They were really delighted to see you, Dad.

After dinner that evening, I joined Uncle Michael as he fed the calves and milked the cows. He was always whistling a tune – a low, quiet sound as if whistling through his teeth – as he slowly sauntered to the barn. There were very few words from him but that felt okay.

The next morning, we called over to see Auntie Tessie and Uncle Dan, who lived on the farm across the fields. Tessie was your youngest sister and, again, what a beautiful woman she was, always laughing with a happy twinkle in her beautiful green eyes.

What a brilliant holiday we had, Dad. It was the first time in my life that I really got to know you.

We talked about the history of the Northern conflict, you told me many stories of ghosts that appeared on Rathlin, we laughed and we even sang old Irish songs together.

I will carry the precious moments I had with you for those two weeks in 1976 in my heart always, Dad.

Thank you for everything. I still miss you.

BARRY GERAGHTY

Champion jump jockey Barry Geraghty is a winner
of the Grand National and the Cheltenham Gold Cup.
He is a native of Co. Meath.

In the Moment

From twelve or thirteen years of age, I was into the horses. I left
school a year early. I did a riding instructor course, which got me
out of my Leaving Certificate examination. It was only a smoke
screen to allow me to follow my passion in life. It's great to go after
your passion in life, no matter where it takes you. I've been lucky
enough; it worked out for me.

The downside of my job is that I have unsociable hours. I get
very busy, and when you're busy, the simple life is what you long
for. I'd be racing horses over in England for maybe five days in a
row, and when I'd get back home, my two kids would come in from
school, and all I'd want to do is lock the front door. I'd just want to
spend time with them at home. There's nothing more I love than to
go out for a bite to eat with my wife and two children, or simply
play with the kids. The simple things.

I would see lots of people, be it in racing or in everyday life,
who struggle with the highs and lows, but I see myself as a
positive person, a glass half full person. I'd never get too high, and
I'd try never to get too low. I'd try and keep things normal. That's
why I enjoy the simple life. I love it. Today, I've been in the farm
all morning, and yesterday too. I make it happen when I can.
There's a peace of mind with the simple life. Everyone has

stresses or things hanging over them, but worrying about them won't make them any better.

How I handle worry has a lot to do with my job. Preparation for a race is limited. You have to have your weight right; you'll study the opposition's form, but you can only get your preparations to a certain level. After that you have to stay in the moment. In certain cases, say, like a big race, you'd maybe subconsciously be going through the What Ifs, and, without letting them weigh heavily on you, you would be going through scenarios, but, with experience you know the scenarios, so you don't need to go through them. It becomes second nature. Our game is the opposite of a lad standing up in a match to take a penalty. You don't have time to think. When the tape goes, everything is in the moment; how your horse takes to that first fence. He could charge at it as if it's not there and pay no attention, or he could be there and he could be focussed and the two of you are on the one wavelength because it's all about a partnership. You want to get working together. So, you can't really do a whole lot till you sit on that horse. And it's how you click. And then you just have to constantly re-assess your position in a race. You know, to say that it's "tunnel vision" is correct in a sense but, actually, it's everything. You're just taking it all in, in the moment. That's why you can't get too bogged down in a lot of the What Ifs. You can only deal with it just as it happens. I think it's a good way to be.

At big meetings, you can have a bad result in a race, but the next race is equally as big, so you can't let the past affect the present or the future. You have to say "It's gone. You screwed up there, now let's not screw up this one!" You need to be determined, but there's no point in being too determined because you can't force it either. You need to work on what you have. If you think of a horse-race as being a marathon, then you are in trouble. If you think, "Right, I did a bad time over the last marathon, so I'm going for this!" and you go flat to the boards, by half way around, you're gone. You need to find the balance: pace, judgement – everything comes into account.

I've been lucky with the people for whom I've ridden all through my career because they'd always say, "Move on, Barry!" and I'd be the same, so they've been lucky too. It's important to move on.

There have been plenty of good days, but there have been days when results didn't go my way, or I fell off a horse, things went wrong, but the people I've spent my career riding for would be fairly philosophical about it. They wouldn't be beating me up. I wouldn't beat myself up either. "Win the next one. That'll put it right." That's how I would always be. The truth is I get very little from negativity. I get more from positivity, so I try to focus on the positive. There will be times when I'm going to be negative, of course, but there's definitely something to be got out of being a bit more positive about something, and trying to work forward rather than going over and over the past. I know that there's nothing to be gained from beating myself up.

If I was very down after a race, I would look towards home: it'd be my two children and my wife. "You have that," I'd tell myself. You come back to what's important in life. You appreciate what you have. I come back to the centre, what it's all about. You'd block all the negativity out because you know what you have at home is irreplaceable. That's what matters the most. Take your work seriously, but not yourself, would be one of my sayings. Of course, work shouldn't dictate your life either. Work to live, not live to work, I say. After all, you'd like to go around with a smile and enjoy your kids and enjoy life. And laugh at your cock-ups. I love a good laugh and am a big fan of Des Bishop.

I'm also a big believer in diet and exercise. My wife is a nutritionist. She has taught me a lot about diet. Eating better will affect your form for the better. Sugars will affect your form. If you take a can of Coke, your body is yo-yoing. If your body is yo-yoing, your brain is yo-yoing too. Bad food will affect your well-being, your form, your sleep, whereas a staple diet – nothing fancy – is great.

I'm physically a big enough jockey, so I have to exercise a lot on days off, or even on a day on. I have to lose four or five pound before a race, so I'd be running on the race-track. I love it. It's brilliant. The endorphins are released from exercise. The world's a better place after a run. After a run, you're feeling good and you're a lot lighter. And problems, big or tiny, don't matter so much when you've run forty minutes. I'd also take a lot of supplements for nutrition. Multi-vitamins. They all affect your mental form.

I'll probably go out for a run this evening. A lot of lads sit in a hot bath and sweat it off, but not me. I run the weight off rather than starve myself. I believe in going for a run and eating a good meal afterwards. It works for me. I imagine that when I finish my riding career I'll be still running.

Watch out for me!

NIALL CARROLL

Niall Carroll is a world champion kick-boxer. He holds numerous national and international titles including six world gold medals. He also does boxing and has a national title and at present is part of the Leinster Development Squad. He lives in Co. Kildare and has just completed his Junior Certificate.

What's Your Dream?

At 15 years of age, I don't normally think about the beauty of every-day life. However, having a brother with special needs I don't take things for granted and realise how lucky I am to be able to train and reach a high level in my chosen sport – kick-boxing. My brother is my inspiration. He has to fight battles every day in his life, and he still finds time to wish me luck and worry that I stay safe.

I started kickboxing when I was seven at Combat Kickboxing in Prosperous, Co. Kildare, under Vinnie Murphy. I have won various competitions and Leinster and Irish Nationals titles every year since starting in competitions at the age of 10. I joined Carbury Martial Arts when I was 10 and started entering competitions that year. When I was 11, I won my first World title at the World Karate and Kickboxing Council (WKC) in Portugal taking home two gold. It was one of the proudest moments of my life standing on the podium with the Irish National Anthem playing. My dad was jumping up and down with excitement. I had my picture in the newspapers and all the hard training was worth it. In 2011, I won gold at the WKC in Spain, and, in 2012, I went to the WAKO's in Slovakia and won bronze there. I took bronze again in Poland in 2013. In 2013, I also won 2 gold at the WKC World's, having knocked out three of my opponents in competition. Currently, I box with the Ryston Boxing Club and am on the Leinster Development Squad.

Of course, it's not all plain sailing. Injuries are part of the sport. So far I have broken my toe, two fingers, tore the tendons in my hand, cut my face, which needed plastic surgery, and at the moment have fractured my thumb. I didn't realise my thumb was fractured and continued training. Eventually when I couldn't move my thumb at all I went for an X-ray.

In 2011, I became the Youth Ambassador for the Asthma Society of Ireland. I have exercise-induced asthma and take inhalers every day. I am very proud to be part of the Society and I try to get across the message that having asthma does not have to stop you reaching your goals in sport.

I feel very proud and thankful that I have had the opportunity to do something I love. I am lucky to achieve world standard and be able to travel to different countries to compete. I am lucky to have a family that supports me and a brother that supports everything I do. I have been lucky to experience the proud moment of fighting for my country with the crowd shouting my name to win. I have experienced standing on the podium with a gold medal with the Irish National Anthem playing whilst holding the Irish flag high and proud.

Muhammad Ali, a true champ, once said, 'Champions aren't made in gyms. Champions are made from something they have deep inside them – a desire, a dream, a vision. They have to have the skill, and the will. But the will must be stronger than the skill.' An opponent might be bigger than me or more experienced than me or more successful than me, but that doesn't make me feel that I can't win: I can. Once I start thinking that I can't; the match is over before it's begun. I have to have hope. I've got to believe that it's a possibility. Oftentimes, people lose a match because they've lost before they've begun; they've ruled out winning. Don't rule out winning in life, no matter if you fail. Setting your heart to something is at least half the battle.

Moreover, whatever success is for you in life, go after it with all your might, doing whatever it is you do to the best of your ability –

and enjoy it. When I win a fight, the referee lifts my hand to indicate that I am the winner, but I generally feel nothing because I am still 'in the zone'. It's only afterwards when I'm in the car on the way home chatting with my dad that I actually feel it and appreciate it. You have to step back in life to enjoy success. When I get home, I usually treat myself to a few well-deserved snacks.

Hopefully in the not too distant future I will stand on the podium with an Olympic gold medal. That's the ultimate dream for me.

What's yours?

PAUL DUNPHY

*Described by Marian Keyes as "the funniest person of all time",
Twitter legend Paul Dunphy Esquire is a social media curator
who famously comments on all things twittery – his dog Mindy,
his fella Peter, food, wine and way too much TV.*

The Salad-Spinner of Happiness

I'm as giddy as a giddy-arsed pike, and that is giddy, let me tell you.
(Have you ever seen a giddy pike?) I'm about to meet my Twitter
pal Marian Keyes for the very first time...

Mar – this nickname started when I needed more space in
Tweets – is about to do a rare reading from her best-selling novel
'The Mystery of Mercy Close', followed by a Q&A and one of her
'Glitterin Raffles', which she normally does on-line.

I'm in a fevered state.

We've been Tweeting one another since I started a career-break
and took to the Twitters in my spare time. Soon after I followed her
on Twitter, Mar followed me back, thrilling me to bits. The laughs
have been instant and uplifting. There has been 'craic' and boldness
to boot.

We share a lot of things in common – a fondness for ridey men,
an appreciation of a good chocolate bar (Wispa for me; Twirl for
her) – and the wrapper, good eyebrows, and Strictly Come Dancing.
(Aljaz for me, Pasha for her.)

And now the Queen of the on-line 'Glitterin Raffle' herself is
about to walk in through the doors of Smock Alley. It's almost too
much to bear. I can barely contain my excitement. Typically, on

Mar's on-line Twitter Glitterin Raffles, the Twitter machine does be close to breaking as so much activity takes place, the highlight being when Marian calls out the winners 'live'. But this is different. This is a first – a real life raffle in front of an audience. She has even DM'd me on Twitter to tell me in advance where to buy the tickets for the event because I have been glued to the computer for days awaiting news of tickets going on sale. And I am going to meet her in person.

And lo and behold, here she is now striding through the door with her very handsome husband Tony! Next thing, her arms are around me and there's hellos and air kisses (so that we don't upset each others' make-up) and warm chat.

It's Twitter with sound. I'm cock-ahoop with glee. One of the most honest, and fun people on Twitter, indeed probably the world's most interactive 'famous' person on Twitter, who chats to everyone, completely unaware that a Tweet from herself brightens up that person's day, has just given me a great big hug and now is chatting to me and I'm thinking this can't be happening. People would give anything to be in my place. Marian Keyes, one of the funniest people on Twitter, whose openness about her mental health issues has encouraged others worldwide to talk openly about their own issues, is chatting to me about anything and everything – how well I look and how great it is to finally meet.

Is this the woman who just the other day Tweeted 'Oh It's Brucie being very funny again #mehole', about Strictly Come Dancing causing me to laugh myself silly because the half of the world that isn't Irish was probably trying to figure out what #mehole meant? I pinch myself. It is. Marian who is brazen bold and brings out the 'worst' in me – not that I need much encouragement – is chatting away with me. I am in Seventh Heaven.

But the reading from 'The Mystery of Mercy Close' must begin. We must take our seats.

A fun and moving reading and Q&A follow – all in aid of the Green Ribbon month to raise awareness for mental health issues, during which Mar is typically open and funny. Then it's time for the live Glitterin Raffle itself. Marian has prepared all the raffle prizes –

everything from biscuits to a nice pen for all her followers who have applied on-line to participate in the raffle.

'There's only one person who, I'm sure you will all agree, can be called on to spin the Salad-Spinner of Happiness tonight and that person is Paul Dunphy Esquire,' she says.

Whoop ahoy! I am cock-ahoop, beaming from ear to ear. What an honour and a joy!

It's a night to remember. I'll never forget it.

Marian picked me out of the crowd in life.

People do that in life. They acknowledge you and bring you along on your life journey. They're called friends – for life. My advice? Stick with them.

Since the Glitterin' Raffle, I've been lucky enough to appear on Tom Dunne's Radio show on Newstalk with Marian, where basically we 'prittle prattle' on about everything and anything, much to Tom's – and hopefully the audience's – amusement.

It's a dream come true.

Heaven only knows what we'll get up to next on Twitter!

Marian focuses on fun and the positive. This I LOVE because when I'm on Twitter I want to get 'away from it all' and have some fun. The world is full of 'bad' stories. It's important to switch off. Marian helps me do this.

Now I must go and see if Marian is on the Twitters...

Join us @PaulDunphy and Marian @MarianKeyes, if you like.

You won't regret it. And, who knows? You might even win something!

LUKA BLOOM

Since 1969, when Luka Bloom (known then by his birth name Barry Moore) set to the stage to support his older brother and renowned Irish singer Christy Moore, Luka Bloom has been bringing his unique, passionate sound to indigenous and international audiences on stages from the United States to Australia. He is regarded as one of Ireland's best-respected contemporary folk artists, having produced 20 albums since the 1970s.

The Man is Alive

He was everywhere that year. My father's shadow was ever-present. He had died suddenly 32 years earlier, at the age of 41, leaving a gaping wound in the house. I was the youngest of 6; how my 33-year-old mother coped is simply beyond me. 'You just get on with it', she'd say.

I have no physical memory of him; I've carried the charcoal portrait of him done when he was 30, in my mind forever. If he were alive today, he'd be 80-something, yet to me, he's a handsome 30-year-old dad.

I left home at 17. Hard to be the son of a great man in a small town, especially when you had no real sense of who they're talking about.

So, there I was in 1987, 33 years old, travelling and working in America. Finding my feet, wings even. Yet, for some reason, he was everywhere around, above, below, beside, and, inside me. No matter where you go, there you are.... And it was a lingering hurt, an inability to accept that unknown. At times I even felt angry, which was irrational, and felt shameful. Someone kindly suggested that you wouldn't be angry with someone unless you loved them. That helped. You just get on with it.

It was October '88, driving from Amarillo, Texas, to Vancouver, Canada. 1580 miles; 50 hours. Autumn trees all gold, red and yellow, shedding slowly. Leaves dropping effortlessly. No sleep, for fear of missing something unforgettable. Just drive, the length of the glorious Rockies. Near Laramie, in Wyoming, I looked out across the big sky, beyond the swaying grasses, and felt a little aching within. I wanted to see the buffalo. For a moment, the road was meaningless to me. Where are the buffalo, the eagle, the wild horses, the wild men and women of these great plains? Shadows now; humming and drumming quietly in the background of our busy little lives. But you get on with it. 2 sunrises and sunsets later, I pass Seattle, and come to the city of Vancouver. I will be here for one day. Love the skyline, love the water, have a good feeling. Meet the people I'm supposed to meet and do my business. Have dinner, and decide to read my book awhile in one of those millions of groovy little coffee shops that now exist all across North America. Mug of hot chocolate, piece of pecan pie, a good book.

Alone, no problem.

And then I saw her.

Long, blonde-brown hair, fresh face, the smile of a happy life. She was looking curiously over at me. Being lost in my little world, I hadn't noticed .

'Are you British?' she asked. 'Are you American'?, I asked. We laughed. 'I'm Irish', sez I. 'I'm Canadian', sez she.

We're laughing.

How is it that certain people meet and instantly like each other?

In a few moments we are sitting together, chatting away, small talk about work, Vancouver, and Ireland. I explain that I'm only in Vancouver for the night, driving to Seattle in the morning.

'Then you must see something special', she suggests. 'You must leave Vancouver having seen something so beautiful that you will be compelled to return'.

'Let's go', sez I. Happy not to be alone for once in a North American city. Happy to have found such a lovely soul.

We climb into her battered Volkswagen Beetle, and, talking at 100 miles an hour, she takes off onto the Streets of Vancouver. I sit back, take in the streets, and her giddiness.

Stanley Park is a Vancouver landmark, a haven of celebration (commemoration?) of Native-American life. Among totem poles on a crisp, clear October evening, we looked out across calm water before us. To our right were the lights and buildings of the city; its shapes and colours dancing in the water. To our left were hills, small mountains.

I'm awestruck by the stillness, the beauty of this place; the strange incongruousness of the city, the water, the hills, the wooden monuments to the ancient North American world. Silence.

'See those lights over there on the hills to the left? That's where I was born and grew up '.

'Are your family still there?' I asked.

'Just my mother', she said.

'My father died when I was one'.

This was such an incredibly magical scene, that when she said these words, I immediately became uncomfortable. Shivery sensations up and down my spine, around my neck and shoulders. Within seconds I wanted to leave , return to my hotel, watch TV, shut this out.

But some little voice within me said be still, be here, it's OK. Hear this.

'What happened to him?' I asked.

'A crash. He was 41.'

'I lost my father when I was one, Glynda. He was 41 also.'

The moon was nearly full, the sky was deep blue. We were speaking softly.

'Isn't it strange to grow up in a town where everybody knows your dad except you?'

'Sure is,' she says, smiling.

We were now into the darkest area of my life; the long shadow of my father, his death too young, the tragedy of his loss to my family; everything that had fed my self-pity.

Glynda was still smiling. Somehow, though our experience had been almost identical, I felt that her life was different from mine,

her way of 'dealing with' this trauma was different from mine.
She was more resolved than I was, more comfortable in her skin.

'How have you coped without your father, Glynda?'

'Oh, he's always been with me, and I've always known he loved me.'

Those six words. I could hear nothing else. Time suspended,
place irrelevant, I was living in those words, and what they meant
for me: 'I've always known he loved me'.

I was 33 years old. How could I have missed it all those years?
Everybody always told me what a beautiful man he was. I knew he
loved them. I knew he loved my mother. How could I have failed to
see how much he loved me?

I had to get to 33, come to America, be alone, drive the Rockies,
meet Glynda, trust her, come to this sacred place, stand still in the
Canadian Autumn breeze, and hear her say those words. She gave
them to me; and right there and then I knew indeed my father
always loved me.

It got cold, we left. I cried, and cried. She understood. We talked
and hugged, and eventually said goodnight. We cracked up laughing when we realised we had the same birthday. It was ridiculous,
but we weren't surprised.

6am, the sun peeps out, and I begin my journey to Seattle. It was
the beginning of a new day. Nothing has changed in the world. But
for me, nothing would ever be the same. And ever since, I have felt
my father's presence with me.

ANN EGAN

Ann Egan has won many literary awards including Writers'
Week Listowel Poetry Prizes and The Oki Prize. She has written
a historical novel, Brigit of Kildare, *and three poetry collec-*
tions, the most recent, Telling Time. *Her poems, broadcast on*
RTÉ Radio, are widely published in Ireland, USA, England and
Australia. Below follows one of her short stories.

The Parting

All winter long of 617 AD Fiachra imagines his leaving. Can he
really leave this home-place of all his seventeen years? Leave his
father who has high hopes for his 'Ree Cohee', his very own, 'Battle
King'? He shivers although winter's pale sun warms his quarters,
warms his garden, waiting to burgeon once more with plants,
flowers and weeds even, garnered from secret hillsides of his
childhood. The tall, dark-haired youth paces the rush coverings in
tempo to his father's fading voice. His eyes, blue as a kingfisher,
darken. Tears roll down his face.

'Poor Father,' he frets to the silence. 'His idea of a battle has
nothing to do with my battle. He's right about my not wanting to be
indoors. I can't bear that. But outdoors, that's my blessing. I want to
live my life under the solitude of God's sky, and move, like my
grandparents did. They followed seasons, trekked the sun's falling
about our lands. But what will Father say? How will he face his
disappointment if I tell him I want to clasp the psalter not the
sword. I want to go to Clonard, study under Finian, not run wild
across the Slieve Blooms with the O'Connors, fighting enemies into
submission. I want to pray, not carouse into the small hours.

Oh God! I can just imagine his face. It will turn to stone. His knuckles will whiten on his sword's hasp. His head will curve downwards. He'll become silent. I can see it all now. He will put his eyes through me. Fling our family sword on the banquet table. Stamp out of our hall.'

Fiachra pulls his cloak closer about him and picks up a small, silver shovel which he has treasured since he was seven years of age, despite his father's protests that a small sword would befit a well born child more. Fiachra strokes its smooth oak handle as if its inanimate companionship might assuage his torment. He looks all about, thinks of his garden, the kingdom he had dug out for himself over the past ten years. He pictures neat rows of foxglove, spring bulbs just waiting to peep over the clay; coppery hued grasses, quiet in the predawn; rows and rows of flowers, plants, vegetables, saplings – all lined up like dutiful children hidden from attention. In the distance, beautiful tall trees offer comfort.

His heart grows heavy with memories and his mother's protestations haunt his resolve.

'Oh, God.' Fiachra shudders. An icy feeling pierces his heart. 'Why is that not enough? Why can't I still these voices in my head? Does solitude never mean solitude? Why can't I simply say: "Mother, you live your life. No one tore your heart asunder to stay here or go there, or marry this one or drop that one. You had your own happy life with my father and your four children. You longed for another son for me to play with, but Mother, my sisters were kind and good and I spent happy hours following them around, taking part in their playing."

'And Father. I know well I'm a sore disappointment to you, going away from home, from all our lands and people. I want to leave before spring comes. Before our fields are set and alive with seedlings ... If I leave you to your old age with no son about you. How, how can I do that? God in mercy! But I want to go, Father. Stay I cannot. How can I marry Deirdre O'Connor as you wish? I've heard Finian preach. Heard God's call in his quiet church, and know I have to answer. I hear your call too, my Father, your call to my heart and soul. "All this will be yours, Ree Cohee," you said to me one day on the summit of Slieve Bloom. "Look all about you, this

will be yours, my son. Halloo!" you cried and off we galloped, tore
down the mountainside, heather and gorse and wild berries flew
past us, faster, faster, father and son, racing as one to our destiny. Is
my destiny your destiny? I want so much to go my own way.
Forgive me, Father for what I'm trying to do.'

Dawn's yellow beams break. Fiachra looks all about his quarters.
He steps outside. He gazes beyond to the garden. A frown mars his
fresh, open face. He gazes at the great home and at the bell that tolls
the day's duties. Searing pain gathers. How much longer can he live
like this? He is certain his heart must shatter. He is a kind and good
person but as the holly bush must lose its berries to wind and bird,
so too is his tolerance and forbearance forsaking him.

He loves this ancient place, he loves his own father and mother
and three sisters. How can he leave? All their people, the old
gardeners, trees, stones, and his garden, and go?

Go!

He falters as he walks beneath the gate's archway. Dawn's last
beam strikes the old bell, its coppery glow expands. It resembles a
guardian angel. Tolls him a soul song:

Go. Fiachra. Keep going.
Many before have left.
Many more will leave.
Each must walk his way.
In leaving you will always stay.
In staying, you will go forever.
The silver wind is on your back.
May its blessings go with you!

Fiachra's footsteps quicken. The infant sun casts granity glints on
yesterday's rain-pools. They lap the song of peace to the rhythm of
fading footsteps.

A young man leaves.

Fiachra carries the earth's blessing with him. He goes on his
way, strengthened by his ties with his family and his friends. He
knows he will carry his memories and their consolations with him
always, wherever he may go.

CAROLINE FINNERTY

Caroline Finnerty is a mother of a five-year old daughter and two-year old boy-girl twins from Co. Kildare. She is the author of 'In a Moment', 'The Last Goodbye' and 'Into The Night Sky', all published by Poolbeg. She is currently busy wiping noses and working on her next novel.

Cuddles

If you had asked me at the age of twenty-two 'So where do you see yourself in ten years time?' I don't know what I would have answered to be honest, but I'm pretty sure that fishing turds out of a bath-tub definitely would have not been have been on my list. Nor would cringing while a four-year old roars with excitement in the aisles of my local Tesco 'Look mama! You have them at home!' whilst pointing at the Tampax.

Or realising I have forgotten to take off the pink sparkly necklace that said four-year old insisted I wear when leaving the house.

Changing at least four nappies by nine a.m. Every morning. Without fail.

Being on the edge of hysteria when I find one twin carrying a bottle of Cillit Bang and the other a bag of Caster sugar – even though I have press locks.

Trying to make dinner with eighteen-month old twins hanging off a leg each like people clinging to a palm tree during a natural disaster.

Climbing over the bars of a cot and curling up between Mickey Mouse and Barney just so I can get some sleep too.

Declaring that 'nights out just aren't worth it anymore.'

Trying to restrain my inner control-freak when the red and blue Playdoh get mixed together. Similarly resisting my OCD need to sharpen all my daughter's colouring pencils to the same length.

A trip to IKEA where your four-year old wears safety goggles the whole way around – you're not really sure why but hey, she's happy.

Getting annoyed by the father in Hansel & Gretel because he chose the stepmother over his own children.

Getting excited when I see a train/bus/plane going past only to realise that the kids are all asleep in the back of the car and then feeling a bit cheated.

Using a potty in the car-park of Tesco (not me obviously).

But what I also could never have imagined when I was twenty-two is this:

The feeling when a little head finally gives up the fight against tiredness and nestles into the warmth of your neck. Your neck – no-one else's. Open mouthed kisses with juicy wet-lips. Hearing the wanting-cry of ma-ma-ma when they fall. The first cuddle of the morning when it is still dusk out as a little person climbs under the duvet and slots in between your arms. The warmest of cuddles – feeling like you could actually break them because you want to squeeze them so hard. The surge of pride when you watch them sing a song they've learnt or performing in their ballet show. Holding the small pudgy hand of a bouncing four-year old as you walk along the footpath.

The vulnerability you feel when you realise that these little people who drive you demented at the best of times, carry your heart, your hopes and your dreams with them forever more.

Such is the beauty of life.

MARIA DUFFY

Maria Duffy lives in Dublin with her husband and four children. It was only when she turned forty that she had the courage to follow her dreams and pursue her writing more seriously. She's published four books with Hachette Ireland in the last three years and is currently working on her fifth. Maria says it's a constant juggle, being a mammy and a writer, but they're the two best jobs in the world. Below follows one of her short fiction stories.

The Streets

Knives slashing my face. That's what the December wind feels like as I walk across O'Connell Bridge. An icy rain has started too, just to add to my discomfort. I'm feeling really off kilter today. As if somebody has taken the thoughts from my head and muddled them up. Yesterday I felt some hope. But not today.

I pause for a moment and peer down into the murky River Liffey. It looks menacing, and yet strangely inviting. I've stood here a number of times this last year and wondered what it would be like to allow the water to take me. To sink into oblivion. Peace. Nothingness. Gone.

I move on. It's time to go home. As I step onto Grafton Street, it seems everyone is going in the other direction. People are coming at me and I'm swimming against the tide. Story of my life.

When I was a kid, my mother used to take me into town to see the Christmas lights. She'd buy me a jam doughnut and I'd lick the sugar off while we queued to see Santa in Switzers. I can remember the happiness almost bursting out of me. But now I hate the lights, and the sight of carollers with their Santa hats, taunting me to be happy. They're just reminders of a time gone past and what could have been.

I'm almost home now. When I reach the enormous Christmas tree at Stephen's Green, I count my steps. Two, four, six... It's silly, but things like that have become important to me. Like holding my breath for a minute before I eat something or blinking one hundred times before I close my eyes for the night. ...fifty-four, fifty-six, fifty-eight. Home at last. It has to be fifty-eight steps. I'm not sure why, but since I got it into my head, it can't be anything else.

I used to be happy. I had a job, a family, a life. I rode the Celtic Tiger like so many others and was on top of the world. But then came the recession and the fall of the mighty. I could say I was a victim of the crash. I could say I was unlucky. But the truth is I was stupid, selfish and made bad choices. I have nobody to blame but myself.

Today I am alone. I am nothing. I am homeless.

I try to ignore the stares of passer-bys as I set up for the night. Bit by bit, I take my bed from my rucksack – a blanket, a sleeping bag, extra clothes. These are the hardest months on the streets. The nights are so cold that sometimes I wonder if I'll ever feel my fingers or toes again. I place an empty cup by my side as I snuggle into my bed. I used to be too proud to beg but I learned quickly that pride doesn't win any prizes on the streets.

From my bed of shame, I watch the world go by. I remember my mother saying: 'There's nothing as strange as folk'. How right she was. Most give me a wide berth or even cross the street. And those who dare to walk close to my bed, rarely make eye contact. I suppose I would have done the same back in the day.

I just want to sleep now. I need to stop the thoughts from whirring around and around in my head. My eyes finally begin to get heavy when all of a sudden, there's a hand on my shoulder and a big booming voice echoes in my ear.

"Howareya John. Hungry tonight, are ya?"

It's Conor from the homeless charity. He's on his hunkers beside me holding out a cup of steaming hot soup. I suddenly realise I am hungry and gladly take the cup from his hand.

"It's gonna be a cold one tonight, John. Do you need anything else?"

I'm acutely aware of his hand still on my shoulder and that's all I need. A bit of human contact. It's like a magic medicine that suddenly brings me back into the world of the living. He doesn't know it, but Conor keeps me alive. His nightly visits reignite my passion for life and make me think to the future.

"Thanks, Conor. I'm grand. See you tomorrow night?"

"'Course you will, mate. Stay strong."

I watch him drive away in his van and I'm filled with hope. Hope is what will get me through the night. Perhaps tomorrow my mood will dip and I'll find myself back in that dark, lonely place. But I know tomorrow night Conor will be back to breath new life into me.

A sense of calm comes over me and I know sleep will come. I start my blinks... one, two three, four, five...

PAUL GALVIN ✔

Kerry footballer Paul Galvin is founder and editor of
www.thisispaulgalvin.com, a fashion and lifestyle.
He can be found at www.thisispaulgalvin.com,
on Twitter @pgal10, on Instagram @pgal10 and
on Facebook – Paul Galvin.

The Big Things in Life

I look for reasons to be happy. I take pleasure in the small things in life, which I guess makes them the big things really. I start everyday grateful for how fit and healthy I feel when I get up. The peace and quiet of where I live also brings me happiness. The independence of my work brings me freedom, which in turn brings me great happiness. I knew that I would need this freedom in my work life to be truly happy. The more I give thanks for these things, the more grateful I feel, the happier I feel. Imbuing in yourself a sense of gratitude for all the good things in your life, however small, is the surest path to happiness that I know. Make the small things the big things and be thankful. If you can't find them maybe you're not looking for them?

MARY KENNEDY

Mary Kennedy is the presenter of RTÉ's Nationwide.
She has four children.

Family Ties

The love and the bond that came into my life the moment each of my four children was born will never be lost. They are the first thing I think of when I wake and the last thing I think of before I fall asleep at night. I have fed them, clothed them, ferried them, laughed with them, cried with them and for them and watched them grow up and become adults who are forming their own lives. We have shared ecstatically happy moments and deeply sad moments and of course because I'm their mother, I worry about one or other of them constantly. It goes with the territory! Motherhood is a most precious gift. It is the best thing that has been given to me and I know I'm not unique in thinking that. From the moment your first baby is born your life is transformed. There are ways in which motherhood is pure delight.

> All that I knew of heaven
> I saw in my babies' eyes.

Those lines are from a poem called The Witless Mother by Belfast poet Emily Orr and certainly there are ways in which I became "witless" when my first baby was born. Motherhood can be overwhelming, exhausting, demanding, but never boring! The fact that I have given life to four people, minded them and nurtured them is the greatest privilege and honour for me. It's beautiful, or as they would say themselves, it's "awesome". And it is.

Now that my children are adults, I cherish the moments I spend with them. I love to cook for them, to go to the cinema with them, to just be with them. I am beside myself with excitement at the moment because the youngest of them, (my baby!) is coming home from abroad next week for two weeks holiday. As soon as Lucy graduated last year, she decided she'd like to travel. So, at the ripe old age of 21, she took off, on her own, to South Korea to teach English. She was the first of her siblings to leave Ireland to work and I thought my heart would break as I watched her turn away from us and walk through security at Dublin Airport. The sadness was compounded by returning home and going into her empty bedroom and opening her wardrobe to see a row of empty hangers. I felt so so lonely and I know her brothers and sister missed her hugely too.

The beauty of everyday life though is that Lucy is having a stimulating and interesting time in Korea and has made great friends from different parts of the world. We keep in touch constantly thanks to Skype, Facebook and Facetime and I was proud as punch when I visited her last October to see how mature she had become, living and working and embracing a new way of life. And of course, we have the joy and the excitement of her homecoming next week. It'll be one big party lasting two weeks. Then there'll be the sadness of leaving her to the airport again and watching her back disappear through the security gates but then both happiness and sadness are part of the rich tapestry of life.

While my children are definitely the centre of my universe, there are so many other ways in which the beauty of life is manifest to me. I love the colour of the sky, the way it changes. I can't resist taking a photograph of a beautiful sky and tweeting it! I find the colours and textures uplifting and I hope people who see the tweet will be similarly impressed. I love the wind. There's nothing I enjoy more than a good walk on a windy day, inhaling the fresh air, blowing away the cobwebs and feeling re energised. I love people. I love cooking for my friends, going to the cinema, just being with them.

Oops! I'm having a *déjà vu* here. Isn't that what I said about my children at the beginning of this piece? It holds true in all situations for me.

> It is a sweet thing friendship, a dear balm,
> A happy and auspicious bird of calm.
>   *Percy Bysshe Shelley*

PETER HANNAN

Fr. Peter Hannan SJ is a Jesuit priest who writes on the themes of Christian spirituality and love in the everyday. He has written eight books, including The Search for Something More, Follow Your Dream and Love Remembered. All eight books have been published by Columba Press. His website is www.peterhannan.ie. Peter lives in Dublin.

The Great Beauty

Sometimes I love nothing more than to sneak away from my writing-desk and take in a film in the Lighthouse Cinema, in Dublin.

Recently, I went to see The Great Beauty. The film tells the story of Jep, a man about town who lives at the centre of Rome's night life. He works as a journalist and is seen as a connoisseur of the highlife, knowing everyone who matters but he is gradually becoming politely disenchanted with life. He is ready for something more when he is visited by someone who married the woman he first fell in love with. His visitor revealed to him that his wife had recently died and that going through her belongings he had found her diary. On reading it he discovered that Jep was the one she had been in love with all her life. In the light of this, Jep began to reappraise his life in relation to love, sex, society, art and Rome. He realised that he had turned aside from 'the great beauty' he could have found in life. Compared to the beauty of this experience, he feels that all else is so much rubbish, but that seen in the light of it everything has a new radiance.

Literature and movies are full of our experiences of our dream of love and of how its beauty or splendour draws us into a relationship with others in which joy prevails. Being the second last of a family of ten children I have never ceased to wonder at how my brothers and sisters were grasped by love's beauty and transformed by it when they fell in love and turned from being difficult teenagers into affable adults.

Few have expressed the extraordinary power of beauty to transform us as Shakespeare in his 29th love Sonnet.

When, in disgrace with fortune and in men's eyes,
I all alone between my outcast state,
And trouble deaf heaven with my bootless cries,
And look upon myself and curse my fate,
Wishing me like to one more rich in hope,
Featured like him, like him with friends possessed,
Desiring this man's art and that man's scope,
With what I most enjoy contented least;
Yet in these thoughts myself almost despising,
Haply I think on thee – and then my state,
Like to the lark at break of day arising,
From sullen earth, sings hymns at heaven's gate;
For thy sweet love rememb'red such wealth brings
That then I scorn to change my state with kings.

Over the years I have had a profound interest in the centrality of beauty to our human dream and I have written much about it. Its power never ceases to astonish me. When I studied Philosophy to become a priest I became aware that from very early in its history Philosophy concluded that we see reality, as through a prism, in three very distinct ways: as true, as good and as beautiful. While what is true and what is good were reflected on exhaustively during my years as a student-priest, what is beautiful, sadly, hardly received a mention. Slowly, I began to see beauty as an essential part of the human dream as it is the intense attractiveness of the love that creates and sustains the main relationships of life and the joy we find in them. My brothers and sisters were proof of that. Beauty is to be found above all in the love exchanged in our relationships with family and friends. Like the poet William Wordsworth, we tend to seek beauty initially in nature and in art but fail to find it where it essentially is in love.

Vain is the glory of the sky,
The beauty vain of field or grove,

> Unless, while with admiring eye
> We gaze, we also learn to love.

In this context, the great psychologist Erich Fromm's comment in his book, The Art of Loving, is poignant. He says that the greatest and yet the most neglected art in life is that of loving. There is a unique style of relating, a presence and aura that each of us develops in our efforts to communicate love. It is a style of relating we need to notice and appreciate, first of all in ourselves, for if we do not find it in ourselves we will not find it in others. It can easily be missed because our finest hours are often the most ordinary. The writer John McGahern captures this well when speaking of his childhood:

> I am sure it was from those days that I take the belief that the best of life is lived quietly, where nothing happens but our calm journey through the day, where change is imperceptible and the precious life is everything. (John Mc Gahern – Memoir)

There is a touching example in the film Calendar Girls – another of my favourite films – of how a person has learned to notice this kind of 'art' and its beauty in his life. Jim who is terminally ill with cancer speaks to his wife of the glory he has seen grow in her over the years of their marriage. He says to her, 'The women of Yorkshire are like the flowers of Yorkshire; every stage of their growth is more beautiful than the last; but the last phase is always the most glorious'.

For me, what makes these words truly striking is that, at a time when we no longer associate beauty with the way people relate to one another, a man would notice the glory in his wife's life and be willing to express it so eloquently.

All of us are innately attracted by the radiance given out by people who are grateful for the past, joyful about the present and enthusiastic about the future. Anything we can do to help people to become aware of and to believe in what we admire most about them, as the Jesuit poet Gerard Manley Hopkins puts it, that their lives 'are charged with the grandeur of God', is the greatest service we can do them.

It's never too late to tell someone that you love them – and tell them why.

CARMEL HARRINGTON

Carmel Harrington is an author living in Wexford with her husband Roger, and children Amelia & Nate. Her novel Beyond Grace's Rainbow *(published by Harper Collins) won both the Kindle Book of the Year and Romantic Book of the Year in 2013. Her second novel* The Life You Left *was published in June 2014. Carmel has also written articles for The Irish Independent, The Daily Mail, The Evening Herald and Woman's Way. You can find Carmel at www.carmelharrington.com.*

Breathing in the Beauty of the Day

Tom Ellis moves at a slower pace these days. He pauses and thinks for a moment. When exactly did old age catch up with him? He looks in his bathroom mirror, assessing himself with a critical eye. A shock of white hair frames his heavily lined face and eyes once denim blue are now faded to a pale grey. He raises his hand to his head and salutes old age – a crafty bugger, in truth a worthy adversary who works hard every day to slow him down – silently swooping in to make creaking bones groan and crack in protest and pain.

'I may have lost the battle, but the war is not over yet!' Tom declares defiantly to his image in the mirror. Then chuckling at himself, he begins the ritual of shaving and washing.

In his 73 years, Tom has never left his house unshaven, just one of many legacies bestowed to him from his father. A memory floods his mind, that of his beloved parent standing at the kitchen sink, with Tom standing between his two legs, watching in awe as he skilfully moves the razor blade 'swish swash' across his chin. With a final pat of aftershave on his now smooth face, his father would look down at his son, ruffle his curly hair and say, 'Always start the day as if it's a special one, Tommy boy. Because you never know, it might just turn into an amazing one!'

So now like his father before him, Tom washes, shaves and dresses before moving downstairs for his breakfast ready to accept whatever magic the day might have for him. He walks around the spotless house once again to make sure it is tidy. He then opens the fridge and smiles in satisfaction. It was heaving at the seams, laden with every kind of possible treat that Mary might fancy later that day. He intended to spoil his wife when she came home. He looks at the kitchen clock and worries that Billy might be late. But before he has a chance to fret, the doorbell alerts him to his son's punctual arrival. He rushes to open the front door, gathering his wallet and keys as he goes, then picks up the bouquet of wildflowers that he has bunched together with tin foil, smiling as he anticipates Mary's face when she sees them.

'Morning Pops,' Billy says to him when he opens the door.

Tom beams with pride at the man standing before him. From the very first time he held him in his arms, a new-born all soft and wrinkly, he felt his heart explode with love and pride and now thirty seven years later, that same feeling assaults him whenever he sees his son.

'Hey you shouldn't have Pops!' Billy teases his father as he sees the flowers. 'For me?'

'Get away outta that!' Tom replies laughing heartily. 'They are for your Mam as well you know.'

As a soft breeze washes over him, he pauses at the front door and closes his eyes to inhale springs breath. The sweet, fresh, fragrant aroma of the flowers from his front garden, coupled with the slight musky smell from the dew on the grass, assail his senses.

'You OK Pops?' Billy asks with concern.

'Just breathing in the beauty of the day, that's all son.'

Tom eases himself into Billy's car and they head towards the hospital.

'Listen to this Pops, got it for Mam for the drive home.' Billy pushes the CD play button and Puccini's *O Mio Babbino Caro* fills the car up.

Tom leans back into his seat and closes his eyes to allow the vocal purity of Kiri te Kanawa to envelop him. As always with this song, he is immediately brought back to his wedding day and like it happened only yesterday he can see his bride Mary, walking down the aisle towards him, to this very aria. Billy knows better than to speak right now, he grew up listening to Puccini and when this particular piece came on, both his parents would pause whatever they were doing and look at each other, and without saying a word, the love between them would take his breath away. This song was a sonnet of love for them both, a musical love letter, and a monument to their devotion.

When the last note finishes, Tom opens his eyes and pats his son gratefully on his knee.

'You did good with that, son.'

'Not long now Pops & Mam will be home again.' In all their years married, they'd never been apart for more than one night. So it had been difficult for them both, each worrying about the other.

Billy looks at his father and suddenly decides to confide in him, 'I'm going to propose to Alice.'

Tom starts to laugh with delight and soon as is often the way with laughter, it spreads, so Billy joins in and tears are coming from both their eyes.

'Your Mam is going to be so happy!' Tom declares and cannot wait to see Mary so that they can tell her.

'I want what you and Mam have,' Billy says earnestly.

Tom pauses, and then closes his eyes for a moment to gather his thoughts. 'You have it already son. I can see that when Alice walks into a room and your eyes light up in recognition as you move towards her. Don't ever forget that feeling. Stay up late the odd time and eat dessert for dinner. Laugh together and cry together when you have to. Always kiss each other goodnight and good morning and no matter what craziness is going on in the world around you, stop and close your eyes and inhale in the beauty of everyday life all around you.'

Billy blinks back tears and knows that he will never forget the wisdom of the words just spoken. He says nothing for a moment, until he switches the car engine off.

Taking his father's hand, he looks him in his eye and nods, a silent promise to do as his father has done before him.

'Let's go get Mam.'

GERALDINE HUGHES

A native of Belfast, actor Geraldine Hughes has received many awards. Among her stage credits is the West End production of Jerusalem, which she also performed on Broadway. Her television credits include: The Blacklist; Blue Bloods; Nurse Jackie; Mercy; The Good Wife; Law & Order CI; Law & Order SVU; Law & Order; Murder, She Wrote; The Celtic Riddle; ER. Geraldine has starred in several feature films including Gran Torino, Rocky Balboa and Dead Souls. She has also appeared in Killing Lincoln.

The Wonder Woman Stance: A Power Pose

I heard this recently on a TED "ideas worth spreading" talk. The idea is that even if you don't feel powerful or unafraid, with a shift in your body, you can change your position from 'un-powerful' to POWERFUL.

I am going to practice the Wonder Woman stance (hands on the hips, chest up, chin up, looking ahead) for two minutes and will be right back. Go ahead and do it with me. See you in two minutes ...

... Do you feel more empowered? Did standing tall make you feel a little more powerful?

I do. Who knows how long it will last but isn't it wonderful that it can take only a short amount of time to stop and shift your body thus shifting the rest of your day?

How you see yourself is everything.

When I'm Wonder Woman, I instantly become mindful of who I really am.

As I get older, I go slower, and the slower I go, the more mindful I become and thus more generous. Generosity is one of the magnificent off-shoots of mindfulness.

I live in New York City where everyday life is at a fast pace. If you stop for too long, someone will take your space...on the street, on the subway, in the line at the grocery store ... they will get the cab first. It's a race here every day and in the city that never sleeps, I try to find a time every day to stop and breathe and be grateful. I become mindful of my life.

I am very, very, very lucky that I get to live here and make my living as an actress. My fella tells me I have earned my luck.

I live on the 53rd floor of a New York high rise with my beautiful family – my fella, a wondrous Irishman who is my prince, and our chocolate labrador, Abe, who we adopted seven months ago from Animal Haven, a New York City shelter for stray and/or injured dogs and cats.

We have no hesitation stating that he is the most handsome dog that ever lived. We cannot walk two blocks without a person smiling or even stopping us so they too can share in the wondrous joy that he brings. He evokes a reaction in people that is astonishing. A few grown men who work on nearby Wall Street have been brought to tears when they see him and eventually reveal they lost their canine anam cara (soul friend) and miss him or her terribly.

Abe is a very special dog. Even those around us who have their own dogs, tell us that he is extraordinary. I am so grateful that every day we wake up, we have this beautiful creature to love. He was abandoned as a puppy and we had the privilege of giving him a home. We all got lucky.

I tend to think that I live my life with much more resilience than I ever did before as a result of slowing down and becoming mindful of who I really am and where I am in my life. Not to say that I don't have my blue, low self-esteem days where I live in the dark place. Days that are full of "what ifs" and "How come I am not there or that person or have those things?" We all have those moments, those times, those days, but thank goodness I don't live in them for too long anymore.

I used to. My childhood was a poverty stricken war zone in Belfast. My high rise then was in a concrete jungle, surrounded by guns and soldiers and those damn rats...the ones that would run up and down our hall, the ones that covered the streets in the dead of night and ate from the over flowing rubbish bins. They were nasty and big and plentiful. I used to have nightmares that they would make their way upstairs ... I don't know how, but they never did. Now I live with New York City rats and when I see them on the subway platform or roaming like giant dogs across Washington Square Park, I am not afraid of them. I see them as other living things who inhabit this place along with the millions of people. They are as much a part of New York City as the yellow cabs. My perception of everything has changed since those childhood days that were lived in in constant fear....I was afraid of everything and everyone. There was no hope. Where you live should not decide whether you live or whether you die, as the frontman of U2 sings ... and he is right. It shouldn't. It didn't.

I got out and I changed things.

We are all capable of changing our situation no matter how hopeless it seems.

Sometimes it does not turn out the way we originally planned but wherever you go, there you are. If we have people to hug, and who love us, and who let us love them right back ... that is EVERY-THING.

And acceptance is a huge part of that.

I got out of the war and worked until I couldn't stand some days. I went to school. I travelled to a far off land, as far away as I could get from the childhood war zone.

Here I sit in my high rise, with the rats many floors below... much more unafraid.

I can be Wonder Woman when I want.

All I have to do is put my hands on my hips and stand tall for two minutes.

Anything is possible.

ROBERT HEFFERNAN

Robert Heffernan is an Irish race-walker and holder of the gold medal at the World Athletics Championships 2013 for the 50-kilometre walk. He is Cork Person of the Year, 2013. He is married to Marian Heffernan, herself an Olympic athlete. They live in Cork.

The Crunch

I had a coach when I was a young athlete. He wanted to hold me back from competition. I didn't agree with him. I thought he was stupid. I was like a briar. I'll show him, I was thinking. But he was right. Holding me back until the time was right made me hungrier for success and it made me a stronger person and a better athlete. When I won a gold medal in the World Athletics Championships in Moscow in 2013, he was the first person I rang. He was over the moon for me. And the funny thing is, Mr. Hayes, as I still call him now, was not a runner himself.

What does that tell you?

It tells you that sport is about people. It's about what you've got inside. It's about who you are. I had to mature. I had to learn to know myself, and I did, gradually. I would have burned out had I gone too early. You could say that I had to learn to live life. It was a long road. Indeed, these days, there are still days I question everything about myself. At the beginning of 2013, for example, I had the worst start to a year ever. I had the flu. I was thinking, if this continues I'll never make the European Championships. 'Rob's having a breakdown,' my brother-in-law, who is a sport's coach, said to my wife. My wife, herself an Olympic athlete, took it all with a pinch of salt. 'He'll be fine,' she said. 'Let him rant. He'll move on.' I ranted and let it out. That's the way I operate: I surround myself with good people whom I can trust and I let it all out. That way, I never stay down for long.

And, believe me, I have reasons to stay down.

Life wasn't easy when I was growing up. By the age of 10 I was working in a farm picking potatoes. By 12, I was working with my dad, a plasterer, on building sites. Times were hard. I had to work and self-educate myself all along the way. What's more, I developed late. I was five feet three inches in height at Leaving Certificate. I almost fell through the cracks on the running front. At the age of 18, I enrolled for a PLC class and I ran for my school. In 2005, at the age of 27, I was training for the World Championships, but I was still practically living like a hippy, living off my sister for breakfasts and dinners.

I had to work at myself to get to where I am.

The biggest asset of all in life is to believe in yourself. My mam had a vision for me and my sisters to better ourselves and make a living for ourselves, which was fantastic. We were lucky as a family. We were grounded. In a race, when the crunch comes and it's really tough, you have to believe in what you are about. You have to know that you have it inside. If you are bluffing, you'll crack.

The reality is you have to go through the really tough situations because they are what give you that glue. Naturally, it's a constant battle. The front part of the brain is full of clutter, but the deep back of the brain is full of confidence. This confidence builds subconsciously. It is built on experience. It's the difference between reading something and knowing it, and knowing it from experience. When you know something from experience, you've got substance.

I'm coaching a young fellow at the moment called Luke. 'Have you any tips for me?' he asked me the other day. 'Yes,' I said. 'Be honest to yourself and true to yourself. That way you'll come over as being impressive.' I used to hate it when my young sporting friends would take off to the USA and come back a few months later with "the accent", all changed. How can you be the best in the world if you have no confidence in yourself?

In my late teens, I was awarded a running scholarship. Gradually, I was exposed to more and more experts, but a lot of what you need has to come from yourself. It's about the decisions that you make. Two roads diverge, and you have to make the right choices. When I was young, I didn't always make the right choices. I tell Luke nowadays that he can hit the town on a Saturday night if he wants, but that he will have to write the following two days' training off. I know that from experience. I've burned the candles at both ends. I'd be training hard at altitude in the French Alps and I'd head off on the lash with my friends of a Saturday night. We'd go out and drink pints and have a laugh and expect to be the best on the track the next day. We had no fear of training hard, but we had no coach.

Four-times Olympics gold medal winner and three-times World Champion, race-walker Robert Korzeniowski turned things around for me. In Edmonton in 2001 I came 14th at the World Championships. 'This is good result, but for you this is not so good,' he said. He knew that I was doing something wrong. The basics were wrong. It took a few years for me to turn things around, but I managed it. I think if people can do the basics in life, they can do very well. It's about choice and responsibility.

These days, I could be walking around thinking I'm God, with all the adulation people are giving me for being World Champion, but I can't. I have to remember that I am just an ordinary person. Alright, my dad thinks he's famous because people keep coming up to him in the street to congratulate him, but, joking apart, I know I have to keep my feet on the ground and remember who I am. I'm putting my achievements to good use and providing for upcoming athletes like Luke. Besides, I still have goals to achieve myself.

Everybody can be the best that they can be. All they have to do is listen to their personal experience.

IMELDA McGRATTAN

Imelda McGrattan is Regional Facilitator at Kerry Business Women's Network. She coaches and mentors people in how to create more effective relationships and generate short term through long term goals in the marketplace. She is a contributor to Wise Irish Women, *stories of successful, inspirational women who have a connection to Ireland. Imelda is married and has five children and three grand-children. She lives in Dingle, Co. Kerry, and writes poetry at the drop of a hat.*

The Wizard of Oz

One of my favourite films from childhood is The Wizard of Oz. Dorothy has four companions on her journey – Toto, her loyal dog, the Tin Man with no heart, The Lion with no courage and the Scarecrow with no brain.

We women, making our way in what appears to be a Man's world at times, sometimes feel like the Tin Man; we lose heart juggling our home, kids, work, family, friends, and we need a little more time.

So, just like the way the Tin Man got a Ticking Heart, we always need to reserve and conserve a little time for ourselves, to acknowledge our Heart and not lose it in the daily activities that can become so routine.

Likewise, each morning, like the Lion, we women have to master up the Courage to face each day anew. I know, we are rarely praised or given great big Golden Medals as adults to celebrate our strength in the face of adversity, our courage to stand up for what's right for us and those that belong to us, but usually each day, we look fear in the eye at least once.

When you climb into bed at night, remember that, and be grateful for the courage you showed that day and pray for the courage to continue your journey the next day.

A lot of us women, no matter how well we are educated, knowledgeable or informed, may feel like The Scarecrow, quite stupid at times – fearful of asking questions, fearful of standing up to the mark.

But let me tell you, never give up on speaking up. Each of us sees the world through different eyes and perspectives and each of us is entitled to our own opinion and to be heard. As we extend that courtesy to others, so we must teach others to extend it to us.

My life with my children has mirrored the Wizard of Oz musical in so many ways!

It has been colourful, a long and winding road, full of fun, terrors, heart-stopping moments and side-busting laughter among other things. Through my children I learned that I have a big heart, that they see me as the most courageous Lion they know, and that even though I didn't get a University Degree, that was OK because I taught them the things that mattered most in life, namely values, promises, common sense, manners, emotional intelligence, social responsibility and open, honest communication skills. I tailored what they needed to each individual personality, something our schools can't do. Only parents can.

And my children have given me a return that is greater than a Gold Medal, a Certificate or a handsome Ticking Timepiece. They have shown respect, love and admiration. All the stuff that money can't buy!

After all this time, at 48, with 5 grown up children and 3 grandchildren, I don't really need to see the Wizard any longer. I don't have a question for him.

I know how to take care of my heart, I know my courage will be there to face each day and I know I will find the answer, when it is needed.

I know all this, because my kids taught me to have faith in me and they don't really even realize that – just yet!

GABRIELLE LOUISE

An American citizen and musician, Gabrielle Louise's ancestors hail from Williamstown, Rathvilly, County Carlow. She has 100% independently released five records, Journey (2006), Around in Circles, the E.P. (2007), Cigarettes for Sentiments (2008), Live in Coal Creek Canyon (2009) and most recently, Mirror the Branches (2010). She has played music all over Ireland. She is winner of the Jack Maher Song-Writing Award and a two-time John Lennon Song-Writing Contest finalist. You can find her at www.gabriellelouise.com.

Blue Skies

Renee, 85, has lived on the upper west side for 25 years. Before that she lived on the Upper East Side for 35 years. Before that she lived in Cleveland. She took one look at New York City and never wanted to leave again.

Now she's sitting by the picture window in a coffee shop on 86th and Amsterdam, tearing her favourite articles out of the New York Times. She folds them neatly and tucks them into her purse.

Five minutes later she takes them out to read again, unfolding slowly, intentionally.

She spots me looking for a free table. "You're all dressed up for a concert!" She exclaims, taking note of my guitar. "Join me!"

And so I do.

Renee puts down the paper and stares out the window blissfully – "People don't know how lucky we are," she says, shaking her head, crossing her arms against her chest. "Look at that! Would you just look at that sun crawling across the building! Look at that blue

blue sky!" she unfolds her arms again and gestures wildly with both, conducting a street symphony.

Although you can only see a sliver of it through the canyon of apartment buildings, I have to notice that the sky IS bursting with saturation this afternoon.

Renee's wearing a black velvet hat from the 1980s and oversize square glasses that magnify her eyes marvellously. Wisps of hair fall out in soft curves, tickling the collar of a red sweater as she whips her head around, taking it all in.

"Just LOOK at those beautiful people in their beautiful clothing, and all the bright yellow taxis, and THAT, will you look at THAT?!?" She points to the glowing bricks on an old church.

"I took one look at New York City and never wanted to leave again." She says, almost to herself.

I'm not sure what to tell her except that The Big Apple has never welcomed me with such youthful enthusiasm.

She gets up from our table and stealthily fills her purse with something from the fix-it-yourself-coffee-station. Returning she leans in close to my face and unfurls a poker-hand of honey sticks. "These are good snacks!" she says. "And free!"

"May I have one?"

Oh, yes, she says. "You get what you ask for, you know."

85 year old Renee in the black velvet hat and the square glasses squeezes my hand and gives me two.

"Enjoy them!" she exclaims, walking away to make friends of another stranger.

And so I do.

PETER McVERRY

While working as a priest in the Inner City in Dublin, Fr. Peter McVerry SJ encountered some homeless children and opened a hostel for them in 1979. He subsequently opened twelve more hostels, three drug treatment centres and ninety apartments. The organisation he started has now been renamed Peter McVerry Trust. He has written about his experience in a book The Meaning is in the Shadows. *His most recent publication is* Jesus – Social Revolutionary?

Butterflies

I received a lovely letter recently from a young boy with 100 euro enclosed. In the letter, he said that he had been saving up all year to send this to us at the Peter McVerry Trust because he couldn't bear the thought of someone having to sleep on the streets.

Some years ago, I received another lovely letter from a 7-year old boy, with 50 euro enclosed. He said that he had just made his First Communion and he wanted to share the money he received with other children who were less fortunate than himself. Five years later, another letter came from the same boy with 100 euro enclosed. He had just made his Confirmation and again he wanted to share what he had got with less fortunate children.

Other letters come from elderly people, often in their eighties and nineties, who enclose 5 euro, with apologies that, because they are living on the old age pension, they were unable to send any more.

The beauty of everyday life lies not only in the giving, but in the compassion and caring of so many people, which the giving expresses. Both the giving and the caring which it expresses are most often hidden from public view. Typically, the beauty is in the small but private acts of reaching out, the cigarette shared, the offer of a shoulder to weep on. Indeed, the most beautiful gift we can give to each other is the gift of our time, the time to sit and listen, to visit a neighbour in hospital, to allow someone to share their pain with us, to sit with a neighbour over a cup of tea.

I see the beauty of everyday life in homeless people and those with addictions and those living in poverty who struggle every day against adversity. The mother who goes hungry so that her children can be fed; the sacrifices parents make so their children can go to school, no different from any other child, with their uniform, school books, and voluntary contributions; the drug user's determination to continue on the extraordinarily difficult path of recovery, in the face of so many setbacks and lack of support, so that they can again become a good parent to their child; the homeless person who can manage a smile and a thank you despite their awful and sometimes seemingly hopeless situation. Their struggle to retain their dignity in the face of rejection and marginalisation is heroic. We rightly admire those, like Nelson Mandela and Aung San Suu Kyi, who so publicly struggle to defend the rights of the poor and rejected. But the greatest defenders of human rights are the poor and rejected themselves who struggle each day to affirm their rights and their dignity in the face of so many obstacles and so much opposition. The beauty in their lives and struggle is almost always hidden from mainstream society.

I remember, as a child, sitting on the grass, on a lovely summer day, and watching a beautiful, multi-coloured butterfly flitting from flower to flower. It reflected for me the beauty and glory of God. It did this simply by being a butterfly and doing what butterflies do. It didn't have to achieve anything, it didn't have to be successful – whatever that might mean for butterflies! It just had to be a butterfly. And then I thought: if this butterfly, just by being a butterfly, and doing what butterflies do, reflects the beauty and glory of God, how much more do we human beings not reflect the glory and beauty of God, just by being a human being and doing what human beings do – getting up in the morning, having a cup of coffee, sweeping the floor, feeding the child, walking the dog.

In these simple, everyday activities, we witness the beauty of life. When we identify the beauty of someone's life by their achievements and successes, as our culture almost compels us to do, then we introduce a hierarchy in the way we value people and their lives. And those with few achievements, such as homeless people, or unemployed people, or people with addictions are relegated to the bottom of the hierarchy. And then we fail to see the beauty in their lives.

How can we describe the beauty in their lives? How can we describe the beauty of a sunset? It cannot be described, it can only be experienced.

You want to know where to find the beauty in life? Look at any teenager, who has fallen madly in love, locked in an embrace with their lover, an embrace they wish would never end. In that embrace lies the beauty of life.

ROISIN MEANEY

Roisin Meaney's books include One Summer, Something in Common, *and* Love in the Making. *Altogether, she has had ten adult novels and two children's books published, and she's made the Irish top five fiction list three times (with one number one). Her books have been translated into several languages and two have been published in the US and Canada. Roisin currently lives with a cat in the west of Ireland.*

The Boy Next Door

I have a boyfriend. His name is Tom. He's blond and blue-eyed and he lives right beside me, along with his parents, two brothers and a sister.

Tom and I became an item about a year ago, when he appeared at my window one day. I opened the window and enquired as to what he wanted. 'I want to come in,' he said. I agreed to a visit, and since then he's been turning up on a regular basis.

Our dates are uncomplicated, and take place in my house or garden. They last about fifteen minutes on average, and usually involve some form of refreshment. When Tom gets a car we may travel further afield, but since he has yet to have the stabilisers taken off his bike I feel we may be in for a rather long wait.

Tom is four going on five. He's smart and inquisitive and his favourite things, in no particular order, are beanstalks, spiders, his Dad's digger (Dad's a builder) and Halloween. He's also an inveterate daredevil – his parents live in terror of his next escapade. He wandered out from our cul de sac onto the main road when he was barely three and was on his way to the local garage (to get chewing gum, apparently) when a neighbour found and returned him.

When his father asked him how he thought he could buy gum, or anything, without money, Tom replied that he was going to tell the garage man that his Dad would be up to pay later. All sorted. On another occasion he was discovered in a nearby garden pond. Yes, in it, along with the bemused goldfish.

His father has nailed an extra board above the gate of their side passage, to prevent Tom from climbing over. I'm waiting for the day that his chubby face will appear over it, smiling triumphantly. That's my boyfriend.

Of course, there's also a dark side to our relationship. I'm sorry to report that Tom is a bit of a kleptomaniac. Happily, he's also totally transparent. I found him lately coming out of my bedroom (he's long since had the run of the house) with something clutched in his fist, and a guilty-as-hell expression on his face. I prised open the fist and discovered one of my sleeping tablets, the latest in a long line of attempted robberies.

We've also had our falling-outs. He went home in tears once because I wouldn't give him my glasses. (Reading, not wine.) He got a tongue lashing when he aimed carelessly in the bathroom once and flooded the floor. We didn't talk for two days after he found and ate the liquorice allsorts I'd hidden in a kitchen drawer. (I *love* Liquorice Allsorts.)

But overall he's a sweetie. Last Valentine's Day I got my usual quota of cards from male admirers. Yes, that would be none. But on returning from town later that day I opened the front door to find a melted ice-cream on a stick sitting on the floor (luckily still in its plastic wrapper) and a page on which was written, in wobbly crayon, to Roisin from Tom, and a line of kisses and hearts.

He'd posted me an ice-cream. I poured it into a glass and drank every drop. I love my boyfriend.

LIAM LAWTON

Liam Lawton is a composer/performer specializing in sacred music. He has recorded a number of collections to date and his songs have been translated in a number of languages and recorded by Irish and international artists. He is the author of two bestselling books and works as a Roman Catholic priest in Carlow.

A Tiny Cry

It's Christmas and the story is told and retold in Carols, Cribs and Cards. The simplicity and vulnerability of the first Christmas is almost lost in the tinseled tidings posted through our doors and winter frost is re-imagined in designer fashion, while angels like super models adorn the corners of winter skies in waiting.

Not far from Bethlehem another story is being told that I have been following these days with the Associated Press. It's December and the harsh winter winds blow across the plains of north west Syria near Kafer Rouma. It is an ancient ruins that once housed market places, bath houses and temples for this ancient and rich civilization, but now stone upon stone becomes a hiding place for displaced villagers who seek shelter from the bombardment and shelling by Bashar Assad's forces during the country's civil war.

A whole village has moved in, to seek shelter amidst the boulders and ancient walls that once housed the elite of northern Syria. At midnight a young woman goes into labour, and beneath the shadows of stone gives birth to a tiny child ~ a little girl they name Fatima. She is wrapped in swaddling clothes and is protected from the midnight chill and cold winds that blow across the northern plain. All the villagers come to gaze on this tiny child who knows nothing of the horrors that continue around her beyond the walls. Powerless though she may be, her birth is a gift to the community, paradoxical as it may seem. Now all the talk is not of bombs and bloodshed but of keeping the child safe and well. Young men and old shepherds unite in the goodwill of safeguarding the innocent. The gift of life in tiny outstretched arms calls a response from all – the preciousness of life can never be outweighed by the call to revenge and hatred. Every child deserves a chance to live and little Fatima deserves to run free among the orange groves of Syria's summer – even the young and old widowed women who sing lullabies know this.

It's winter, and in eastern skies, shine stars that hang like diamonds on winter plains, the same stars that shone from a Bethlehem sky, where another tiny child was born, – to teach the world of the beauty of life. Would that we would never forget!

ADRIAN MILLAR .

Adrian Millar is a stay-at-home father with three daughters. Until recently, he was the author of Dad's World, *a weekly stay-at-home dad column in The Irish Examiner. He has written two novels,* The Quiet Life *and* Tomayto Tomahto, *and one book of non-fiction,* Socio-Ideological Fantasy and the Northern Ireland Conflict. *He has two PhDs, one in Japanese and one in Politics. You can follow Adrian on Twitter @AdrianMillar.*

A Tsunami of the Heart

A journalist phoned me the other day. "I see from your blog that you've been a stay-at-home dad for the past thirteen years.
I wonder if you have any tips for men who are suffering from the economic downturn and are finding it hard being stuck at home all day with kids.'

How long have you got, I felt like saying, but instead I launched in headfirst as is my wont when I am speaking about things close to my heart, like family.

So, I told her that I chose to give up work as a lecturer in Japanese the second my wife got pregnant on our first child, and I regretted it every Friday morning when I opened the jobs section of The Irish Times.

So, I quit buying the paper.

I told her that my wife never wanted me to give up my job because it would make her look like a 'bad mother', and I grew resentful.

So, I went to marriage counselling and worked things out.

I told her I felt like a twat standing in the school-yard watching mothers in their 'power suits' drop off their children before heading on to work, and me, a man with two PhDs, going back home to change nappies.

So, I took to writing while the kids watched Barney.

I told her that I was called 'the wife', 'the yummy mummy', 'Mr. Mum', by those around me, and was told that my wife wore the trousers.

So, I learned to believe in myself as a father.

But, of course, it didn't happen overnight.

When my first child was born, I stood there patiently waiting till the midwife handed her to me. When my second child was born, the nurse wrapped her in a blanket and I immediately took her in my arms and smiled for the camera. When my third was born, I grabbed her and held her to my chest like a rugby ball, crying out "My daughter! My beautiful daughter!", regretful of the fact that I had been mildly disappointed at our 20-week-scan when she wasn't a boy, because I had desperately wanted a boy to be my shadow as I had been my father's, and now I knew that I wouldn't change her for the world.

I lined three bottles up in her cot night after night because she was the last of our 'litter' and we doted upon her, and I'd wake in the morning to find her with a million bits of soggy nappy stuck to her hair and body, the nappy having exploded, but I told myself that she was worth it. I called her from a friend's house the other day. 'I am going to buy you a puppy for your seventh birthday,' I said, finally caving in after five years of pressure. She screamed hysterically, dropped the phone and ran off down the house while I fought back tears on the other end of the line.

'If there was a tsunami in our village, would you run to the hills for safety?' her sisters asked me recently.

'No,' I said. 'I would run to the school to get all three of you first, and we'd probably all die together.'

They looked at me like I had two heads.

'Really?' they said.

Really.

What parent wouldn't?

Parenting is the greatest and most beautiful job in the world. No job requires more skill, more creativity, more responsibility and imagination, more self-belief, more dedication, more energy, more commitment, more backbone and more resourcefulness, and no job is more rewarding.

'And the day men recognise this,' I told the journalist, 'is the day they stop feeling a sense of loss.'

Actually, any woman could have told her that.

BRIDIE MONDS-WATSON (SOAK)

Bridie Monds-Watson, is the 18-year-old Derry singer-song-writer SOAK. She has supported The Undertones, Snow Patrol and Chvrches. Her EPs Sea Creatures and Blud are critically acclaimed. In 2013, The Observer described her as 'one to watch'.

Expect the Unexpected

When I was younger I was often shy and self-conscious about how I felt. I kept most things to myself. This made me angry and frustrated a lot of the time. It probably wasn't pleasant for those around me and I guess it hurt them that I didn't feel comfortable enough to explain my actions. What I needed was some sort of outlet, a way that I could get problems and anger out of my mind without being obvious because talking openly made me feel weak and vulnerable.

Surprisingly my outlet came along in the form of music.

After attending local gigs I asked my dad to teach me guitar. There was something about observing live music that I soon found addictive. It made my heart race and put a smile on my face. I felt like I'd finally found my 'thing'.

Just like everyone in their early teens I was desperately trying to figure out who I was, what made me, me. Music was bringing me closer to understanding that. The more I listened into the lyrics of a song, the more I was learning about the artist and how they felt when they wrote it and the more I learned about myself.

Usually I would give up on things easily if I wasn't good from the outset but I felt like I had to be good at music. My love for it made me refuse to throw in the towel when it came to learning an instrument. The only other time that I can remember being so determined was whenever I was about five years of age and my school-teacher realised that I had severe dyslexia. My parents were told that I'd probably never read or write and that I should probably be sent to a 'special' school where I'd be given the help I required. For years I spent weekends doing extra work and going to the 'reading Centre' outside of school, eventually it all paid off, by primary 7 I was in the top English class and years later I passed my English and English Literature GCSE's. It was quite unexpected but my parents believed in me and I believed in myself.

When I became fluent enough in playing guitar I slowly started writing songs (they probably didn't sound any good, mind you). I found huge comfort in writing. For the first time I could comfortably express myself as I always wanted to. I could get everything out of my head and onto paper. Details that I didn't want to explain, I was able to hide within unobvious words so others could make their own meanings. I loved writing songs. I was finally shrugging weights off my shoulders and finding my own voice, literally.

The next step was to showcase a few songs to someone that wasn't myself, so I sung my parents a few and they thought they were quite amazing. They weren't aware that I could sing or write songs, so I guess it was a nice surprise. I was sharing my feelings through music and it made me feel OK about being open and honest.

Everyone that I played my songs for really enjoyed them and couldn't believe I'd written them. This gave me confidence to share my work with wider audiences. I began by putting my stuff online and playing at open microphones. I guess a lot of people liked what I was doing because my whole musical 'career' just kept getting bigger and bigger. I kept getting gig offers and I kept recording. Radio stations started to play my music. I was slowly building up a local audience/fan-base. The more I played the more my confidence grew. Others were finding comfort in my music and that made me realise that it wasn't just me that felt how I did when I was writing those songs. I didn't feel like such an outsider.

My career continues growing. I've signed a publishing deal and a record deal. I've released two EPs and I've a third one coming. I've now toured with artists who I listened to when I was younger, who first taught me what music really meant. I spent last summer doing the Irish festival circuit with all my friends. Soon I'll be doing more tours. I can't wait to get back on the road again and see so many new places, meet so many new people and learn so many new things. I'm extremely lucky to do what I do. I literally live life to the full, and you should too.

Music worked for me, but if you look hard enough you'll find what can help you. I learnt that once you express how you feel, scary as it may be, you'll never look back. Life is full of unbelievable opportunities. Make sure you're here to take them.

Live everyday like it's never going to be repeated and never look back.

Expect the unexpected.

SINEAD MORIARTY

Sinéad Moriarty was born and raised in Dublin where she grew up surrounded by books – her mother is an author of children's books. To date, Sinéad has had nine novels published by Penguin. Her books have been translated into 25 languages. Her latest novel is called The Secret Sisters Keep.

Resting Place

Jenny looked out the window. It was lashing rain, no surprise there. It hadn't stopped raining for a month. She turned away from the window. It didn't matter about the weather. She had been dreading today. Ever since her mother died they had been arguing about it. Each sibling had their own opinion of how it should be done.

Each sibling had very definite views of where it should take place. She thought it was incredible that three people could be so completely opposed in their views. Each of them claimed to know exactly where it needed to happen. Each of them was convinced that they were right.

It had taken weeks of negotiation for them to come to this compromise. Jenny had been disappointed that her choice hadn't won through. She knew that she was the one who had been closest to her mother.

Her younger sister, Anna, claimed that it was her, but Jenny knew that was a lie. Her mother had spent half of her life giving out about Anna – how selfish she was, how thoughtless she could be and how disappointed she was that she never married. She also thought Anna's children were wild, 'feral' she had called them once after a particularly bad weekend spent in their company.

Her brother, Oliver, thought he was closest to their mother simply because he was the only boy. Granted their mother had put him on a pedestal but that had all changed when he married Abby. Her mother had hated Abby. She had never said it outright, but Jenny knew from all the snide comments and criticisms her mother had made – Abby was a snob, she was lazy, she was foolish, she was a spendthrift...the list was endless.

According to Jenny's Mum, Abby had corrupted poor, innocent Oliver. He wasn't 'the same' anymore. He was 'different' and it was all Abbey's fault. Jenny disagreed. Oliver had become an appalling snob all by himself. Ever since he got that new job he seemed to think he was above everyone else.

Jenny knew she was the favourite. After all, she was the one who called into her mother the most, talked to her the most and cared about her the most. It was Jenny who had found their mother lying in the back garden, gardening gloves and secateurs in hand, dead.

Jenny was the one who had arranged the cremation. Oliver had been too busy and Anna had been too traumatized. After doing nothing, they then both had the temerity to criticise the ceremony.

Suddenly when it came to scattering their mother's ashes, Oliver and Anna wanted control. Oliver insisted that she be scattered on the hilltop where they had walked when they were children. Jenny only ever remembered going there once or twice.

Anna wanted to scatter her mother's ashes in the sea. This was utterly ridiculous as their mother was terrified of the open sea and hated boats.

Jenny knew exactly where her mother's ashes should be scattered, in her garden, amongst the flowers and plants that she had so lovingly nurtured and helped flourish. The garden where she had spent so many happy hours forgetting her troubles as she cultivated her oasis.

The compromise had been the forest where they had often gone camping as children. Jenny had agreed but only after figuring out a way to make sure her mother finished up in the right resting place. In the end it was very simple. Jenny collected the urn and poured her mother's ashes into a Tupperware box. Then, she took the ashes from her fire and put them into the urn.

The ashes from her fireplace were scattered in the forest on a miserable rainy day. Then, Jenny went home and waited. On a beautiful clear day with a blue sky above her, Jenny scattered her Mother's ashes around the garden where her mother had been happiest and most at peace in life and now in death.

Now everyone was happy. Sometimes you have to be patient to find the perfect ending. Sometimes you have to compromise to keep the peace. But it's always worth it in the end. Jenny's mum was now in her perfect resting place, surrounded by the nature that had consistently filled her with joy during the ups and downs of her life.

Jenny hoped that she too would find solace and inspiration in nature as she walked through the winding road of her own life.

DONNCHA O'CALLAGHAN

Donncha O'Callaghan plays rugby for Munster and Ireland. Since 2009 he has been Ambassador for UNICEF Ireland. In 2011, he released his autobiography Joking Apart: My Auto-biography. He is married and has three children. He lives in Cork.

A Giant Life Lesson

Along with family, rugby means everything to me, but it's really intense. We train four hours a day and the other twenty hours, you're on the clock: nutrition, rest, monitoring water intake, taking care of injuries. It's all about wins and results. It's high pressure. So, even though I am really privileged to be doing something I absolutely love, I do need to escape sometimes. That's where craic comes in. Craic helps me flick in and out of the intensity of rugby. People expect me to have a pair of clown's shoes on and a rubber nose when they meet me, and that's pretty much what they get.

The other thing in life that helps me flick in and out of the intensity of rugby is UNICEF. When UNICEF invited me to be Ambassador, I jumped in two feet first. I'm a social beast. As UNICEF ambassador, I've been to South Africa, Haiti, Zimbabwe and Lebanon. I have seen things that I never thought I'd see. I was in Lebanon once, two miles from the Syrian border, at a refugee camp, when a mother ran up to me and dropped her baby into my arms. I will never forget it. I was in total shock. It was like holding the 'Live Aid' baby in my own hands. She weighed no more than a pair of tights or a light jumper. Her mother had mistakenly thought I was the doctor. I had always told myself that if anything ever happened to anyone in my family, I would do everything for them, and here she was doing exactly that – in a split second. I was awe-struck at her love for her child. UNICEF got her child to hospital.

We visited another camp the next day. It had been set up as a temporary camp, but three years on refugees from Syria were still living there. You could sense the aggression and the huge frustration in the inhabitants. A group of men approached us as we got out of our cars. I knew from the look of them that they could easily have killed us, but the second that they heard that we were Irish, they melted. They softened. The tension went straight out of their bodies. I was astonished, but our interpreter explained that once they had found out that we were Irish they had relaxed, because the Irish are synonymous with help in Lebanon. I was never so unbelievably proud to be Irish. We Irish are the biggest providers of aid in Lebanon, and our Army serves there as peacekeepers. A lot of people knock the Irish because of the recession but the truth is the Irish are amazing. Compassion is in our DNA, I think, because of the famine. We are really tough on ourselves, but we shouldn't be. We are known all over the world for our kindness and generosity.

The leader of the camp spoke.

"We need water," he said. "I don't care if it's dirty. We just need to drink."

We got them clean water. Some of the children were suffering from water infections. Many of them were malnourished. Some of them had lost their parents. Too many of them had seen incredible things that you wouldn't wish on a child. One 5-year-old boy had seen his mother being beheaded. There was a 6-year-old boy who had gotten third degree burns the previous year when his house was shelled. He still couldn't speak with the shock. I had to look deep into his eyes to see the child that he had once been. They were not the eyes of a 6-year-old.

On another UNICEF trip, to South Africa, we visited another refugee camp. Child exploitation is rampant in South Africa among minors who have been trafficked from Zimbabwe. Maybe because I have three young daughters myself, I noticed how fragile and vulnerable the girls were in particular. Many of the children had no shoes. They used open holes in the ground for toilets and as they had nowhere to play, they would sometimes fall into them. Many of them also had no schooling. In some cases, only one child from a family could go to school, which was 'school-in-a-bus', and that child would then have to teach the rest of the family when he or she got home. The pressure on the child was enormous. We set up games in the camp for the children to try and give them a sense of normality. As they played, out of the corner of my eye I noticed a husband and wife looking on. They hugged each other. They were hugely emotional. It was the first chance for them to see the enormity of their situation. We had lifted the burden off their shoulders just the tiniest bit.

I only really ever take in the enormity of what I see abroad when I have come home to Ireland. When I'm abroad it's like I'm taking it all in 'in slow mo'. When I sit down at home and think about it, I realise how blessed I am in my life – materially, yes, but also in terms of well-being – and how important it is not to lose sight of this. I also realise that when a person is vulnerable, like the people I met in Lebanon and South Africa, they are at their most beautiful because they are at their most real, and it's really humbling to see.

So, you could say that UNICEF has taught me one giant life lesson: never to be afraid to show your vulnerability. There is always someone there for you. People can't but reach out to you.

The Irish are proof of that. Worldwide.

ANTHONY NASH

Born in 1984, Anthony Nash is currently on the Cork senior hurling panel in his position as a goalkeeper. He is also a teacher with a passion for all kinds of sports. He lives in Co. Cork. He has one sister, Edwina.

Family and Friends

I pity the teachers who taught me when I was a boy. I would have done anything but study. Any given chance, I was out the back of our house pucking a ball off the wall. I always wanted to play for Cork. I put the ball through our kitchen window – the biggest window in the house – any number of times. Looking back, I probably did my parents' heads in. Once, I put a golf-ball through my grandmother's window: it went straight through the heart of the picture of the Virgin Mary hanging on it. I put my head down and tried to hide. Hurling was in my blood. My uncles and cousin played for Limerick. My dad drove me hundreds of miles to matches for both club and county. When he couldn't bring me because he was working, my club-mates stepped in and brought me. Eventually, I was called onto the Cork Senior Hurling panel but, being a goalkeeper with only one position up for grabs I had to wait on the sidelines. Some of my friends told me I should rethink my situation and to go to the USA in the summers to play, but I knew that that would rule me out of a place on the Cork team, so I decided to hang on and keep trying. It was frustrating at times because anyone would tell you that when you're involved in sports you just want to play.

In the meantime, I got on with my life. I studied Business for four years at Cork Institute of Technology and then pursued a Masters in Food Marketing in University College Cork. I had to make up for all the years that I had been pucking balls off walls! I wasn't sure what to do with my life, hurling and work. I am a very lucky person as I have a great family who support me in everything I do. Whenever I'd consider stepping down from my position from the Cork Senior Hurling panel my family always encouraged me to dig in, saying that my opportunity would arrive. One year rolled into another and gradually I began to lose hope of ever playing for Cork. The one thing that I wouldn't change from any of those years is the friends I made from all over Cork and outside. At the end of my Masters, I had to decide whether to go out to work or train to be a teacher. I decided to train to be a teacher.

Funny thing is, if I had not decided to train to be a teacher, I would never have played on the college team that year under the guidance of the amazing Paul O Connor. We won the Fitzgibbon Cup that year. Again my family were very supportive of me during this time, especially when I was after spending seven years in college.

In 2012 I played my first year as a starter for Cork. It's a fantastic honour for me to play for Cork. I played in an All Ireland semi-final against Dublin in Croke Park the following year. I ran out into 'the roar' I had never heard anything like it before; it sets your heart racing. I went on to play in two All-Ireland finals, unfortunately losing the replay, but the experience I hope will stand to us in the future.

Nowadays, life has come full circle. I puck the ball with my niece Caoimhe and nephew Micheal. This is something I did with my family when I was their age.

I'm happy with the choice I made to become a teacher. Sometimes students come up to me before class these days and say, 'Sir, can I go to hurling or rugby?' and I say, 'Of course'. They remind me of myself when I was in school. You can't make them study. (I do try.) Besides, you need balance in life. They say that "the devil makes work for idle hands". I think it's true. It's important to keep active in life.

I'm in a good enough position in my life today. I'm happy. I have the support of my family and friends.

While I am not the most patient person in the world, as those same people would tell you, with their help and advice I went the long way around to teaching and playing in goals for Cork.

What can I say except that you can't beat the support of family and friends?

COLM O'GORMAN

Colm O'Gorman is the Executive Director of Amnesty International Ireland. He is the founder and former Director of One in Four, the national NGO that supports women and men who have experienced sexual violence. Colm has also served as a member of Seanad Éireann and is the author of the best-selling memoir, Beyond Belief.

Beauty is to be Found in Surprising Places

I know that I am blessed. I am lucky to have been born with an innate appreciation of and wonder at the beauty of life. I knew it as a child. It saw it, as I grew up on the family farm in rural Wexford. It was there every day, plain for my child's eye to see.

I felt a connection to something bigger than myself, something I was very much part of. I felt it most acutely in nature, in the fields as I walked them; in the summer evenings as I lay on our lawn and listened to the wood pigeons calling from the massive oak tree hear the house. I saw it in people too. In the twinkling eyes of Jimmy O'Shea who helped my dad on the farm and who had known my long dead Grandfather. Jimmy smoked a pipe. I'd sit on the wall next to him as he filled it from his tobacco pouch before striking a match and pulling on the pipe, puffing away furiously to get it going. And all the time he'd talk, and his eyes would twinkle and I'd feel that connection with him and all the people he'd known that I never would, those like my grandfather who were long gone but who lived on in his memory, in the stories he told me.

A lane lined by huge beech trees led down to the farmyard of my childhood home. Those trees were ancient, and their bark was scored with carved graffiti that was decades old. Love notes and messages from those who had trooped down the lane fifty and sixty years earlier, to dances held in what was then my Grandfather's barn. I loved reading those messages scored deep into the grey bark of those huge trees. There were even pictures, like hieroglyphics, carved into the trees. It was history recorded on a living canvas, the stories of those who had come before, those who had walked the same lane and were now long gone. Their lives and loves recorded, waiting to be discovered by the child I was as I ran my curious hands across the bark of those massive trunks.

I knew that I belonged to life, that I was part of a long continuum, stretching back to the very origins of life and forward to an infinite future. That was comforting, and very beautiful to me. It still is.

It also helped me when things were hard. Life is full of beauty, but there is also darkness. I knew the darkness too. I experienced it in terrible acts of abuse as a child. But that deep connection with what was good about life kept me grounded and meant that the darkness never swamped me. I was always able to hang on to my deep conviction that life was in fact good and worthwhile.

That was difficult at times. Often I felt overwhelmed by anger turned inwards into deep shame, and by a sense that there was no way past the ugly horror of my experiences of abuse. At times the pain of that was soul destroying. That was especially true when, aged seventeen, I ran away from home and found myself homeless on the streets of Dublin. But then at my lowest ebb, life, in the form of a kind smile from a passing stranger, would pull me back from the brink. A smile and a look of acknowledgement would capture me, bring me back into connection with life, and I would survive.

And isn't there such beauty in that too? In the fact that we have the capacity to reach across to another, a stranger, and with a simple smile, save their lives by reminding them that they are as human and as worthwhile as the rest of us.

I learnt a lot from that time. I learnt that life is hard, and that it can be overwhelmingly so at times. I learnt that there are times when it seems impossible to imagine it ever getting better. And I learnt that to survive those moments, what I needed was someone to care enough to see me without demanding that I pretend that everything was OK, that my pain wasn't real, and still care about me.

I took that in; it sustained me and eventually, helped to heal me.

Too often when we are in terrible emotional pain, those around us just want it to end, for that pain to lift so that they don't have to bear witness to it anymore. Many people are so frightened of that kind of distress that they recoil from it, or try to dismiss it. They feel powerless in the face of it. And so often in an effort to do something constructive we ask people in distress to focus on all the good things in their lives, on the beauty around them. We need them to be OK, not for them, but because we desperately need them to be OK. We need them to be 'better' because we can't handle their pain. The impact of that on people who are struggling with great distress is often terrible. Instead of being heard and accepted and cared for, they can feel more isolated than ever. It can induce feelings of failure, of shame and terrible guilt. I know this, I felt like that for years.

We really need to develop a culture of acceptance when it comes to depression and despair. We need to accept that there are times when some of us really struggle to see the everyday beauty in life no matter how evangelically it is proclaimed by others. We need to accept that there are times when despair is so overwhelmingly a reality for some amongst us that life seems meaningless. We need to be prepared to hear that and bear witness to it as the truth of the other without judgement or demand. When we do that, we do something incredibly valuable. We do much more than passively sit as a witness to the pain of another. We offer the possibility of an end to the terrible isolation of living in a society that seems to think everyone has to be OK all the time. We let them know it's OK not to be OK.

There is such beauty in life. It's everywhere; in the obvious places like nature, in laughter and joy. But it exists in other, more surprising places too. There is tremendous beauty in the resilience of life, in the dignity and humanity of those who struggle to live with pain and despair. I believe the true beauty of life is to be found in our common connection in it. It exists not only in shared joy and laughter, but in shared grief and despair. In such moments we understand the depth of our connection to each other, we see, in the simple shared reality of our laughter and our tears, that we are one and the same. And in that moment, we share the simple profound beauty of our connection. A connection older and more powerful than all of us, and one full of the limitless possibility of all life yet to come.

MAURA O'CONNELL

Maura O'Connell was lead vocalist with the celebrated traditional Celtic group DeDannan. She has collaborated with Nashville artists such as Jerry Douglas and Bela Fleck, and has been nominated for two Grammy awards – one for Helpless Heart *(released in Ireland under the title* Western Highway*) and one for* Naked with Friends. *She is married and lives in Nashville.*

Luxury

When I wake up, I love to linger in the cozy half-asleep fog that takes form between dreaming and reality. There in the flowing slipstream lies the pleasant fusion of a lovely dream and the feeling of waking up completely comfortable, with a sense of peace and serenity. You can't buy it. It cannot be arranged. I know that because sometimes I have tried to wake myself up with alarms earlier than I need so that I can experience that sense of peace, only to immediately fall fast asleep again after hurling the alarm across the room.

I like morning people. As soon as they are even barely awake, they hop out of bed ready to take on the world. They have lists. They are on top of things. They never find themselves running out the door at the last minute because they have tried to hold on to that heavenly feeling. I have been one myself but given the choice I'll take the bed. For me, this glorious morning reverie is a glimpse of the possible. In this lovely state only good things happen.

The flip side of this loveliness is the mind before sleep. Usually we go over the events of the day in our minds. If we are lucky, it has been a very good one and we are quite proud of ourselves.

Mostly though, we think of things we should have done. We argue in our minds and win the argument thinking of what we should have said. When that argument is won, we then travel to thoughts of the future, mostly worrying about it. What? When? Where? Who? How? All the unfolding drama of our lives comes calling. But the anxiety is part of our lives. The morning makes up for that.

The morning side is, I believe, where the unconscious gives playful tips on life to the conscious mind. I have remembered songs I didn't know I knew there. I have played with melodies and found myself singing the variations on stage without having to think about it because of that quiet peaceful time. I have travelled the world there, and come back in one piece, and it didn't cost a penny. Take the trip once in a while. Enjoy.

PADRAIG O'MORAIN

Padraig O'Morain is a mindfulness teacher and psychotherapist. He writes a weekly column, That's Men, *for The Irish Times. His books include* Light Mind – Mindfulness for Daily Living, Mindfulness on the Go, *and* The Blue Guitar, *a collection of poetry. His website is www.padraigomorain.com.*

A Perfect Day

When he came into money, he set about straightening out the imperfections in his life. First, he knocked down the house. The roof had never really been satisfactory and some of the walls still bore dents from the generations of kids who had grown up there. He built a new house with a perfect, up-to-the-minute design by a celebrated architect.

In the farmyard, the old sheds and barns where he had played as a child had fallen into decrepitude. He replaced them with stables designed by the celebrated architect. Like the house, they were perfect. The stables even had under-floor heating. On the farm itself, old hedges were replanted to give a look of geometric perfection. Makeshift bridges over ditches, railway sleepers installed by his father, gave way to proper footbridges.

Something was still out of kilter. He looked at his wife. She had been with him for quite some time. She had annoyed him by lamenting the changes he made to the house and the farm. Perfection had become his motto and she did not buy into it. Put simply, she was not a team player. The divorce was expensive but then he had the money and perfection comes at a price. His new wife was young but not too young, physically and intellectually stimulating, an excellent conversationalist and had her own Internet business. She featured occasionally, but not too often, in fashionable magazines about the charity she ran in the mornings for Eskimos whose igloos had melted through global warming.

As perfection grew around him, he became conscious that his own days were rather imperfect. He employed a Life Expert he had seen on TED Talks to help him work out a perfect day. The Life Expert cost €2000 an hour. He reckoned it was worth it, though, and reminded himself again that perfection comes at a price. After no more than half a dozen consultations he had his perfect day: early rising, breakfast on the balcony, exercise in the gym, meditation, face time (but not too much) with his perfect wife – the list went on, right up to bedtime at 10pm.

He himself could do with a makeover too, he realised. He employed a personal trainer, a dietician and a meditation master. Before long, he was slim and trim, as healthy as a trout, and he went about wrapped in a sense of calm, like cotton wool.

Then it all began to crumble. He would walk through the open spaces of his house seeing those marks on the wall that had been left by generations of children, though the wall had been knocked down with the old house. He would hear the creaking of a certain step on the stairs that had also vanished. Sometimes he would spot that cracked vase on the landing though it had long since gone to the charity shop. It was the same outside. He would see a non-existent gap in the hedge he used to push through to get from one field to another to another as a child. In the yard he would turn and expect to see the cowshed which had been the military headquarters for some of his games many years earlier. Once or twice he had expected his first wife to open the door and walk in.

Gradually everything started to change back to imperfection. When a new disease began to kill the hedges on the farm he did nothing to stop it. When pyrite ate away at the house and the sheds he ignored it all. If he felt like staying in bed in the morning instead of training, he did so. His personal trainer left. He put on weight. His dietician resigned. He watched reruns of Columbo when he should have been meditating. The meditation master returned to

California. His new wife became appalled at what she had married. Most of the rest of his money went in the divorce settlement.

He became a collector of imperfection. He found he enjoyed doing this. He would go around with a notebook detailing a crack in a wall, a new clump of weeds or a wooden footbridge damaged by a falling tree. if a tradesman failed to turn up he would note that too, not to make a complaint but as another imperfection he had collected during his day. When the perfect roof began to let in water he noted it and did very little about it.

He wondered why he continued to feel restless, though. Was he still hankering after perfection? When he thought about this one day, listening to water dripping onto the kitchen floor, he realised that if perfection leaves you feeling unsatisfied it is not perfection. Therefore, he concluded, perfection does not exist. And as imperfection is the opposite of perfection and a thing cannot be the opposite of something that does not exist, then imperfection does not exist either.

From that moment, he dropped all ideas of perfection and imperfection and relaxed into his ordinary day and his ordinary self. In the neighbourhood his reputation as an eccentric grew all the more strong. Neighbours would snigger when they saw him wandering around the fields or sitting in his window doing very little while the place went to rack and ruin around him. The public health nurse was sent to encourage him to join a cognitive behavioural therapy class in the town but he ignored that too.

He continued to accept himself as the odd creature he was. Finally the neighbourhood accepted him too. He knew they still wished he would agree to improve his life to conform to their ideas of how he ought to live.

But none of that really seemed to matter anymore. He had learned to sink into the experience of one ordinary day after another, and that was enough. In a way, it was nearly perfect.

MARTINA REILLY.

Martina Reilly has written seventeen books, four of which were for teenagers. Dirt Tracks *won a Bisto Book Merit award and was shortlisted for an RAI reading award.* Livewire *received an International White Raven Award. She was also longlisted for an IMPAC award for her adult fiction* Something Borrowed. *Martina also writes plays –* Is this Love? *(An Nuadha Players);* Journey *(Fishamble);* The other Side *(Insight Theatre);* Ten Minute History *(An Nuadha Players). She has written for* Irish Independent *and* Evening Herald *and done a few stints on Liveline's Funny Friday. Her latest book* Things I Want You To Know *is out in paperback. Follow Martina on Twitter @MartinaReilly.*

Heaven

"Mammy, come here quick," my daughter said, her voice low and urgent. "Come and look at the cat."

I immediately had a horrific vision of the family pet lying splattered across the road. I followed my daughter out to a recently renovated flowerbed. "Look," she whispered, in the sort of voice people normally reserve for complimenting new mothers on their off-spring, "look at the cat."

Our cat was stretched out on top of some bedding plants, baking herself on the heat of the clay. As she lay there – I'm not making this up – a butterfly danced past her nose. The cat put out a lazy paw and made a half-hearted swipe at it, way too relaxed to bother chasing it.

"Doesn't she look so happy," my daughter cooed, hunkering down beside her, "I bet you she thinks she's in heaven."

The comment made me laugh. But indeed, if a cat could have a heaven, this was it.

Since then, I've begun to think a lot about heaven. I doubt most people's idea of paradise is sitting alongside God all day and praising him. I mean, a forty minute mass is just about as much as people can take in a week, I don't know how we'd all do it for eternity. And I'm sure God would get a bit fed up with a load of 'yes' men around him.

I asked my daughter what she'd like heaven to be. "I want it to be a place where I am the most popular girl," she said. And then, as a reluctant afterthought, "well, I suppose God would have to be the most popular. But I want to be the second best person and then maybe Jesus."

My husband and son's idea of heaven is one where Bohemians FC eternally beat Shamrock Rovers to win the cup and league double.

I'm sure a doctor's idea of heaven would be to have everyone sick but curable, while a hypochondriac's heaven would be to go to heaven so that everyone would know he really was sick. A mother's heaven is to know that no matter what mistakes she makes, her kids will turn out perfect, while a politician's heaven would be to be surrounded by fat looking brown envelopes. Dancers would go to the great big Riverdance in the sky while all the sinners would be forced to watch it. Plenty of people I know would be happy to go to a great big Lidl in the sky where they could purchase horse saddles, gas grills, satellite dishes and other unnecessary accoutrements whilst doing their weekly shopping. Journalists would love a heaven where every story was a breaking story, where every page was a front page and where every celebrity woke up in bed with someone who was prepared to pose naked whilst spilling the beans on a night of passion. Writers would be in heaven if people didn't say to them, "I got your book and lent it to all my friends."

I had to think long and hard what my idea of heaven would be and decided I'd like to be able to be happy even if I had nothing to lie on but a mound of warm clay. So, yep, I'm coming back into this life as my family's cat.

COLM O'REGAN

Hailing from the small Co. Cork village of Dripsey, Colm O'Regan is a bestselling and critically acclaimed author, comedian and broadcaster. Colm's first two books (the first and second book of Irish Mammies) have both been bestsellers. As a comedian, he has gigged in Ireland, the UK, Europe, North America, South Africa, and the Far East. He writes a weekly column for the Irish Examiner and can also be heard weekly on BBC Radio and RTÉ Radio.

Odd Jobs

The big news in the spring of 1994 was that The Man was interested in renting land from my father. The Man who grew cauliflowers and when the cauliflowers were grown, he hired young fellas to pick them.

On one breezy fresh March day, the deal was sealed. They were talking in the yard, The Man and my father. The Man was sitting in his jeep. His elbow rested on the ledge of the open window, a fag clamped in his jaw which he smoked just with his lips – the original hands-free kit. My father stood about a yard away, absent-mindedly folding and unfolding a docket. It was interesting to watch the two negotiating styles. The Man was direct, abrupt. My father preferred the more circuitous route of haggling whereby he would ignore the original offer and come out with an apparently unrelated statement to buy him some time as he did the sums in his head.

'I'll give you Wan-Twenty an acre for it, Patsy,' The Man said.

[Pause]

'Wan-Twenty begor, Tell me who's building that big house over in across the valley?' my father said.

'One of the Murphys,' –The Man guessing what my father was up to.

'The Murphys. [Pause] You'll do better than Wan-Twenty, will you? Sure I'll have nothing out of that,' my father said.

'Arra feck sake Patsy,' said The Man biting into a Rothmans 'Wan Thirty so.'

'Wan Thirty – begor.'

A car drove past on the road outside.

'Who's that?' my father said.

'Young Sinead McCarthy. The guard's daughter.'

'Is that who it is? You'll go Wan-Fifty will you?'

'Arra blasht it. Wan-Fifty so, ya bollix. I'll be all day here otherwise.'

Somewhere amongst the haggling, my father secured me 'a start' in The Man's yard.

The Yard – that mythical place where boys went at the start of the summer pale and callow and came back as battle hardened young men. Their hands were calloused and boots crusted with soil.

A few months later, I cycled over to The Yard. I loitered uncomfortably while other lads were carted off in different vans and jeeps to the various fields they were worked in. Soon, I was alone, trying to stand nonchalantly.

A familiar jeep hurtled into the yard. The Man roared out the window: 'Cmon away I've a job for you.'

We drove for ten minutes in silence before he abruptly turned off the public road and shuddered the jeep down a rutted country lane.

The lane eventually widened out into the headland of a field of what looked to be young cauliflower.

A flock of pigeons flew up at the approach of the Jeep.

'Look at them hoors ating the young plants,' said The Man in disgust (although the word he used was far worse than hoor)

'Bastards they are,' I said

He paused and looked at me – (Shit I thought, I've gone too far.)

'Bastards is right,' he agreed. We seemed to have bonded.

We got out and stood looking at the fields. The pigeons landed again twenty yards away. One appeared to give The Man the finger.

'Them feckers will ruin this crop. 5 fields of caulifilower and they'll eat every fecking last one of them. And they take no notice of the banger, they're too cute for that.'

Just then the gas banger went off with a gunshot like sound. A nearby pigeon raised an eyebrow feather and continued eating.

I wondered what we were doing here.

The true purpose was soon revealed

'See all those fields right – what you'll do now is keep walking through these fields all day waving your arms at the pigeons to move them on. Never let the feckers settle.'

Without a further word he got into the jeep and sped off. There was no one left except me and the pigeons. Since time began, Man and Pigeon have been mortal enemies gripped in a deadly tango which could only lead to destruction of one or both but despite this, my first day at work as a human scarecrow passed slowly. As did the following six weeks. Each day, I expected Mike Murphy to jump out of a tree with a camera crew, but he didn't. Word got around. Friends ran around waving their arms shouting "Caw Caw" when they saw me. "Bastards" I thought. I preferred the company of pigeons. They didn't judge.

This was not how the summer was supposed to go. I was expecting a rite of passage, not a local interpretation of the Rite of Spring. And yet, the thing which I had at the time seems like a rare commodity now: peace and quiet. Not that I valued it at the time. Any insecure teenager not worth his salt would rather lean against a bus-shelter for 15 hours getting pelted with rain as long as he was with his peers rather than spend ten minutes contemplating the beauty of nature.

But over the course of six weeks, in between patrols around the fields, I read every book in the house. I got invaluable insight into so many fictional worlds ranging from the unravelling mind of a young man (The Butcher Boy) to how a brooding prince might have his heart melted by an unassuming stable girl (a number of Mills and Boons).

It was while reading one of these page-turners, one day that The Man pulled up in his jeep out of nowhere. There was no time to pretend I was working. I was caught bang to rights and to make matters worse, a pigeon sauntered around a few feet away. Sitting in the open air with the birds of the air resting nearby I must have looked like a latter day Francis of Assissi or as The Man put it:

'That's a grand job isn't it? – Being paid to sit there, reading aul shite.'

But he was happy. The unique experiment had worked. Plucky little cauliflower plants had defied the 'rabbits of the air' and were now able to stand on their own one stem.

Although I didn't realise it at the time, the few weeks of bore-dom, books and thinking was like an enema for the brain. And if I could just put down my smartphone and stop obsessively checking it for notifications, maybe I could relive those weeks again every now and then. But without the cauliflower.

ANNE MARIE SCANLON

Anne Marie Scanlon is an Irish writer and journalist who has contributed to publications in Ireland, Britain and the USA including The Sunday Independent, The Evening Herald, Woman & Home, Image, Woman's Way, Prudence and The Irish Post, as well as broadcasting on RTÉ, BBC and radio and TV in the US. Anne Marie is also the author of It's Not Me... It's You! *(A Girl's Guide to Dating in Ireland). For more information www.amscanlon.com. Twitter @amscanlon.*

#DailyGratitude

When I was a child I expected to grow up to be an award-winning actress, the toast of Hollywood and live in a beautiful mansion with a swimming pool. At thirty I was living in New York, defeated, newly sober and wishing for nothing more than a nice husband and a dog. By forty I was a single parent. My son is now seven and there's still no sign of the dog. Or the husband.

I got sober on a Tuesday, sneaking into a 12 Step meeting and hiding at the back. It wasn't at all what I expected, which was middle-aged men, in ancient raincoats, being miserable because they couldn't drink. Instead there were as many women as men, almost everyone seemed extremely well dressed, good looking and, most surprisingly of all, happy.

As the days and weeks went by I heard a lot of these inexplicably cheery people talking about gratitude and being grateful. I wasn't a bit bloody grateful – in fact I was beyond angry. Why me? Why couldn't I drink like a 'normal' person? Why hadn't my life turned out like I'd expected it to? I was smart, talented and not totally uneasy on the eye so why didn't I have a glamorous career, a handsome husband and a safe full of cash and jewels? What had I to be grateful for?

In the decade after I got sober that changed. My life transformed and I went from being the person who baffled people by not living up to my potential to baffling them with my energy and drive. I had an interesting career (with even a small degree of fame), I joined Actors Equity and the NUJ, I had love affairs, I had great friends, a wonderful mother who never stopped supporting me, I lived in New York, I looked good, felt good and was fully present in my life. I had a lot to be thankful for and knew it.

Despite getting sober and truly living I still had a long-standing problem with depression. I was fine for the first two years of sobriety but then it came back, and came hard, as if to make up for the lost time when it hadn't been tormenting me. Over the years, both before and after getting sober, I have tried several things to combat my tendency towards darkness. These 'cures' included, but were not limited to, therapy, exercise, the Atkins Diet, Buddhism, going yeast-free, going wheat-free, self-help books, Prozac, St. John's Wort, prayer, tarot readings, The Secret, Mr Right, Mr Right Now and pretty much whatever fad promised me peace of mind. Some worked but none worked permanently.

Having a child is a game-changer. In my case the game changed beyond all recognition. Before my pregnancy I was starring in my own version of Sex and the City but due to having the worst pregnancy of anyone I've ever known, I ended up as a bit player in Midsomer Murders. When I was three months pregnant I was so ill I was on the verge of a coronary and, as I had broken up with my Baby Daddy, I needed someone to look after me. I was wheeled onto a plane at JFK and wheeled off at Heathrow into the loving arms of my mother. I didn't know it then, but I permanently swapped New York City for a small town in the Thames Valley which frequently makes cameo appearances in the fictional Midsomer universe.

Despite the huge change in my circumstances and lifestyle the first year of my son's life was the happiest I have ever known. But then, when the Young Master was almost two, the Black Dog of depression began to visit me again. On top of the usual misery depression brings I now had the added bonus of feeling guilty for not being a good enough mother. For a while I forgot about being grateful for the things I had and focussed on the things I didn't have. Despite sometimes succumbing to the darkness I always appreciated my little boy and knew I was lucky to be his mother. On the eve of his fifth birthday I wrote on Facebook that in his honour I would post a 'Daily Gratitude' every day for a year. The only reason I went public was in order to ensure that I kept my promise – I don't have a great track record with resolutions. Or commitment.

What I hadn't bargained on was the response. Marking small episodes and little joys as well as big ticket life events struck a huge chord with people. My Daily Gratitudes veered from stuff like getting to travel to amazing countries for work to small things like taking off a pair of pinching shoes at the end of a long day. People commented, posted their own gratitudes and I really enjoyed the whole process. After 18 months, the Black Dog upped his game and I stopped posting.

Strangely enough, not doing my #DailyGratitude (by now I was on an array of social media) didn't help much. Stranger still, people kept asking me to start doing it again. So I did. I'm not a touchy-feely hippy and you'll have to trust me on that, because I know that I sound like one, but having to remind myself on a daily basis of the things we all take for granted – indoor plumbing, clean water, central heating, a free health service, freedom of speech, free education... has helped me enormously.

I don't have a pool or a safe, or an Oscar, but I have a healthy happy child, a loving family, fantastic friends, a dishwasher (I LOVE my dishwasher), cable TV, more books than I can read, my #CorrieBitches on Twitter (fans of Coronation Street), the internet and social media that has allowed me to connect with so many like-minded people and for all these things and more, I'm very grateful. I'd still like a dog, a mansion with a pool and perhaps a husband – in that order. The thing about being grateful for what you have is that there are no limits on what you can wish for.

Try it for yourself – join my #DailyGratitude on Twitter or if you don't feel like going public just keep a private record. It's not a cure for anything except taking life for granted.

COLM TOBIN

Colm Tobin has written and produced a range of TV shows for RTÉ and CBBC. His animated science-themed children's series Brain Freeze has been sold around the world by Aardman Films. He is NOT the writer Colm Tóibín and also not, for instance, Eleanor Roosevelt.

Just Say "No!" to Negativity

It has been on my mind lately, this whole idea of positive thinking. See, for some reason, I've always gravitated towards the negative. I'm not so much glass half empty as "Hey, am I really stuck with this glass? Your man's glass looks much nicer! Seriously, can I get another glass?"

I was a particularly moody teenager. I was a ferociously angry young man. I'm exhausted at this stage, being quite honest.

So, as I get older, I actively try to see things in a more positive light. To be more mindful. See a bigger picture. (I read that Maureen Gaffney book and everything.)

Today, I decided to flick the switch – to finally say NO to negativity.

My usual commute to the office can be fraught with minor difficulties. I like to brew a generous amount of coffee in the morning. Enough for one cup at home and another takeaway cup to tide me over until my first few cups in the office. It's important to stay alert. I've got a stainless steel mug for the job too, which tends to generously soak the upper chest with coffee at every attempted slurp. (I call it The Travel Bastard.) Today, I experience a particularly bad soaking. Normally, this might be an invitation to negative thinking. But not today. Today I laugh it off. "It could be worse," I think. "I could be out of coffee... There could be an EU-wide ban on caffeine... And anyway, isn't this jumper lovely?"

I arrive at the DART station, hoping to make the 8.53am train. Another small hiccup. It's been delayed by 20 minutes. "Poor rail adhesion. Apologies for any inconvenience caused to passengers etc. etc." In my natural state, this would lead to a long string of harrumphs and, most likely, an expletive or two (I once shouted "ya bollocks!" at a ticket machine). But not today. Instead, I contemplate the life cycle of leaves – how they bud in spring, grow luscious and green in summer and fall to earth in an explosion of autumnal colour. And how they then form a layer of gloopy mulch in winter that happens to cause inefficiencies on the train network – and that this is outside of my control. This comforts me somewhat as I stand on the wind-torn platform, icicles slowly forming around my nostrils.

I skip on to the DART as it arrives and set to flicking through news sites on my phone. "Dublin property prices set to soar" the Irish Times cautions. "Conclusive proof of climate change", warns the Guardian. "Beat-boxing baby racks up 8 million views", reveals the Irish Independent. Worried how all this news and static might affect my state of mind, I log off and opt to listen to some music instead. Unfortunately, Spotify won't load because of problems with the 3G network so I decide to have a whistle (the therapeutic effects of whistling are well documented). I settle on Bach's Brandenburg Concerto No. 3, smile at the grumpy-faced passenger in the seat opposite and let rip.

After a few minutes of the most heavenly music, I am rudely interrupted by a passenger announcement – we have to change trains at Connolly Station for "operational reasons". Now I must admit, my initial reaction is to break the window with my elbow. But I re-appropriate this negative energy and instead recall the excitement of train travel when I was a kid and I try to celebrate the fact that I now get to take two in one morning.

We eventually arrive in Pearse Station and I scurry to the door to get off. I am met with a row of students three-deep, barging onto the train. As they maul past me like the Munster scrum, I take a deep breath, bite my tongue momentarily and disembark before the train pulls away. "Things can only get better", I think to myself, before being clothes-lined by a woman on the platform who is texting while walking.

By the time I get to the office, I'm pretty much ready to go back to bed. The heating system is out of order. I've forgotten the charger for my laptop. And there is a pile of work on my desk the size of the National Concert Hall.

But then I notice an e-mail from my Dad. It's a slideshow of photos from a Bike Run he organised in West Cork last summer. My Dad loves his motorcycles and grew up doing motocross with his brother Michael. A number of years back Michael died from a brain tumour and every summer my Dad organises a bike run in his memory, in aid of the local hospice. Riders come from miles around to drive together on a different route my Dad plots out each year – the only rule being that the run starts in Ardfield where Michael was born, go through Union Hall where Michael lived his life with his family and return to Ardfield where he is buried. It's a pilgrimage of sorts – but Dad would never call it that – and it's an amazing celebration of Michael's life and character and their great friendship.

Looking through the photos, I get lost again in that amazing day. As we whizzed through the rolling West Cork hills last summer, I remember having one of those rare moments of clarity. A mixture of real pride in my family, a deep connection with the place I grew up and a feeling of great luck to here in the first place. So this is a place I've decided to return to, in my mind, whenever things get on top of me.

Later on in the afternoon, I experience some irreconcilable differences with a printer – and I knew exactly what to do.

LORCAN WALSHE

Lorcan Walshe graduated from the National College of Art and Design in Dublin in 1978. He has exhibited in numerous solo and group exhibitions in Ireland and abroad and his paintings are in public and private collections in Europe and the U.S.A. He is currently completing and illustrating his first collection of poems.

bordeaux

there is no prayer for protection against beauty
or means to record an exact moment of rapture
when the spirit ventures from veils of caution
and awakens to nature and the grandeur of cities

where the carved stone of civilization is humanized
by the soft light of evening on sandstone villages
and mellow armies of vines halted on hills rolling
beyond the slow river with its history of heaven

glittering on water – an eternity girdled
in a miraculous moment of the tide turning
as the wheel turns on a tsunami of intentions where
we are born as angels running through the tall grass

the shadow of the species shimmers on the margins
an alchemy of daylight glows above the garden
as the malaise of time and the spectre of power
restructure the mind for its journey of longing